SACRED SEX ED

LEOLA
SACRED SEX ED

*FOR PRESENCE,
PLEASURE AND PURPOSEFUL RELATING*

www.talktantratome.com

Copyright © 2024 Lauren Leola Watkins

The author reserves all rights to be recognized as the owner of this work. You may not sell or reproduce any part of this book without written consent from the copyright owner.

First paperback edition May 2024

Book illustrations, cover and interior design by Zuza Miśko

ISBN 979-8-9907089-3-8 (paperback edition)
Published by New Earth Intimacy
www.talktantratome.com

*In devotion to **You**,
for having the courage to traverse your darkness
and embody the full range of your humanity.
For reclaiming your power and
seducing the world into a greater good.*

"PRAISE FOR SACRED SEX ED"

"In **Sacred Sex Ed**, Leola masterfully weaves ancient tantric wisdom with modern life, providing a conscious and transformative alternative to traditional sex education. This book is an invitation to heal cultural programming around sex, intimacy, and relationships. and reclaim the sacredness of your sensuality."
JAMES MCCRAE, ARTIST, POET, & BEST SELLING AUTHOR

"**Sacred Sex Ed** is the answered prayer that the collective has been so desperately needing around sexuality. For anyone who is ready to truly embody their inner tantrika, reclaim their power, and create beautiful, deep relationships that feel divine from the inside out, Leola is the embodiment of this work and I couldn't more of a champion for this book reaching the masses."
MELISSA WELLS, FEMININE LEADERSHIP COACH & BEST SELLING AUTHOR

"This book is a radical gift to our culture's desperate need for a better understanding of sexuality. **Sacred Sex Ed** is an honest breath of fresh air that intersects yogic practice, heart-based intimacy and physical turn-on, leading all of us into a safer, more embodied experience of our own sexuality...and each others. This is a must-read for anyone on the path to full-bodied aliveness!"
MADELYN MOON, SOMATIC FACILITATOR, ARTIST & BEST SELLING AUTHOR

"Leola's work is profound, with a consistent commitment to dive into the shadows and the darkness to unearth personal power. For anyone ready to embark on a deep journey of self-discovery, **Sacred Sex Ed** is the perfect companion. **Sacred Sex Ed** masterfully combines education, Tantric modalities, and practical exercises, empowering readers to connect deeply with their own bodies and desires."
THEA WAYNE, HOST OF SEGGS TALK RADIO PODCAST

TABLE OF CONTENTS:

PART 1	ILLUMINATE YOUR SHADOWS	11
Chapter 1	Turned On By Life	13
Chapter 2	Collective Sexual Trauma	25
Chapter 3	As Above, So Below	35
Chapter 4	Reclaiming Your Power	49
Chapter 5	Trust Yourself	59
PART 2	EXPAND YOUR AWARENESS	69
Chapter 6	Intentional Intimacy	71
Chapter 7	Types Of Sex	81
Chapter 8	Conscious Communication & Radical Honesty	91
Chapter 9	Sexy Consent Skills	103
Chapter 10	Exploring Relating Styles	115
PART 3	LIBERATE YOUR EROS	129
Chapter 11	Discover Your Golden Shadow	131
Chapter 12	Sex Magic 101	141
Chapter 13	Pushing Edges & Upholding Boundaries	155
Chapter 14	Sacred Surrender	163
Chapter 15	Becoming a Pleasure Priestess	173
RESOURCES		183
REFERENCES		187

PART 1

Illuminate Your Shadows

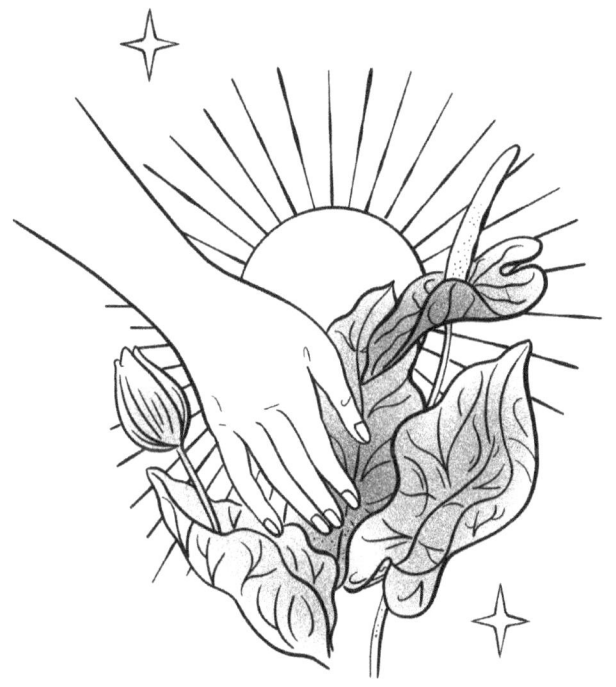

CHAPTER 1:
TURNED ON BY LIFE

This book contains a sex education that the world desperately needs; a sex education that is empowering, honest, and pleasure-based; a sex education that *has the power to end sexual violence.*

I healed from sexual assault using the tools in this book. I repaired my relationship to my body using the tools in this book. I experienced greater depth and intimacy with my partners, friends, and family because of the tools in this book. Studying and applying the principles of Tantra and shamanic sexuality in my life (and subsequently sharing this message with thousands of others) not only gave me the best sex of my life, but also has created evidence of a more loving and connective world.

My worldview has done a complete one-eighty into a more empowering perspective. Where I used to wallow in anger, collapse in fear, and get in my own way over and over again, I now have self-compassion, trust in the universe, and confidence to take inspired action in all aspects of my life. I look at my life's work, founded on the principles I share in this book, with immense pride, knowing it has healed trauma, enlivened marriages, addressed inner child wounding, activated abundance, and empowered individuals to create a life that turns them on.

I'm a survivor of rape along with dozens of other not-so-consensual acts (#metoo), and I've also been on the other side, convincing and coercing partners to be sexually intimate with me. I've let my sexuality rule me.

Control me. Overcome me in unhealthy ways. I wasn't taught how to say "no," nor how to ask for consent. Hell, I wasn't even taught how to *know what I want*. I was mostly taught not to talk about sex.

Sacred Sex Ed has the power to end sexual violence because when you heal your relationship to your sexuality, you start to see it as sacred. You protect it. But you also celebrate it. You share it in healthy ways. You no longer project your sexuality onto others or use it in unconscious and potentially shadowy or manipulative ways. You no longer fear your sexuality, so you actually feel more; beyond experiencing more physical sensation, you also become more receptive emotionally and spiritually. You express more. You become the master of your sexual energy and invest it wisely.

Perpetrators of sexual violence often unconsciously believe the only way they will get what they really want is by force or manipulation. Yet, *Sacred Sex Ed* teaches safe, conscious, and consensual ways to express and explore even your darkest desires. Even more empowering, it shows you how to access the essence of "turn on" in every moment. *Sacred Sex Ed*, built on the foundations of classical Tantra, Neo-Tantra, and shamanic sexuality, invites us to be *turned on by life itself,* by empowering us with tools for sovereignty, creating safe spaces to discover your desires and practice your boundaries. Ending sexual violence begins with self-mastery, especially sexual mastery. This is an invitation to become an ally to the very force that brought you into this world.

Like it or not, sexual energy is the fabric of our existence. It is the most powerful energy on the planet, and simultaneously the most often misunderstood, misconstrued, and miserably underrated. Sex created me. It created you. It created everyone you know. Every human, plant, and animal on the Earth is the product of sex. Look around you now. *Seriously*. Turn your head the full 90 degrees left, and then 90 degrees right. I'll bet that nearly everything you see in your midst was either directly created by sex *or* was created by someone or something that resulted from a procreative act. Sure, some living organisms (such as dandelions) are able to reproduce asexually, but that doesn't exclude them from tapping into life force – it's still sexual reproduction at the end of the day.

And if you're asexual (meaning you do not experience sexual attraction), this book is *for you too*. While I can't claim to have personal experience with asexuality or be an expert in such, this is a safe space to learn more about sexuality with/for a partner or to find tools to process sexual trauma (which most likely affects you regardless of your sexual attraction or lack thereof, as we'll discuss). For a deeper dive into exploring asexuality, I recommend reading Angela Chen's, *Ace: What Asexuality Reveals About Desire, Society, and the Meaning of Sex*.

Sexual energy (also known as life force, jing/qi/shen, and kundalini in various spiritual and cultural lineages) literally touches every part of your life, so when you reclaim and liberate your relationship to it, your whole life changes. You are getting to the root of your existence. Given that sexuality touches us all so intimately, in that it creates our existence and drives us through it, we can see how learning to harness our life force empowers us to create more juicy, expansive realities. When we reclaim our eroticism and learn to channel our life force, we are liberated. We find deep trust in the divinity of life, and thus live abundantly. When we master our life force energy, we are able to bring it into every moment, so that we are *turned on by life itself*.

This is the path I'm on, and I invite you to join me. I have a vision of a world in which sex is treated as sacred; in which we are empowered by our desires, rather than a slave to them; in which we feel celebratory of our nakedness and vulnerability. I dream of world where we can openly and emphatically talk about the energy and acts that brought us into it.

I've created this reality, both in my own life and in the lives of countless others. It is more of a *remembrance* than a revolution. It involves bringing people back to themselves; to their true nature. It comes in three parts, which are mirrored in the context of this book:

ILLUMINATE YOUR SHADOWS.

This involves acknowledging the patterns, authorities, education, and belief systems that have created shame for our bodies and judgment of our sex and have resulted in literally every sexual assault and trauma. It is a journey of healing, trusting ourselves, and reclaiming our power. The journey begins and returns within.

EXPAND YOUR AWARENESS.

Here we discover the magic available when we evoke intention into our intimate lives. We get curious about our vision for relating and gain tools to bring us the most expansive erotic and intimate experiences. The deeper we go within ourselves, the greater our capacity to bring this work into our more intimate relationships.

LIBERATE YOUR EROS.

We are invited to expand our capacity to find pleasure, purpose, and presence in the most unlikely of places. We push our edges and learn how to use our life force energy to manifest our deepest desires. We become evidence of what's possible in terms of living our most turned-on life. We are inspiration for *New Earth Intimacy*.

This is not a linear path. These are not three steps you can check off your list and forever be considered sexually liberated. It is a lifelong devotion to the self and to the betterment of our world. Devoting yourself to this being-ness becomes inspiration for others, which creates infinite potential for a more loving and connected humanity.

By the way, you may be expecting from the title that we're going to be exploring a lot about sexual anatomy, STI awareness, and how to put on a condom, but that's actually not a huge part of my focus as a Sacred Sexuality and Intimacy Educator. If you do want to learn more about these topics from a sacred and/or tantric perspective, I'd recommend checking the resources section for more recommendations.

My journey with sexual liberation was born of my own sexual assault and adjacent traumas. I grew up in a fairly conservative small town in Missouri. Despite the traditional values of my elders and leaders, I was a highly sexual kid. Somehow, I knew what sex was and how babies were made without anyone telling me... maybe it was intuitive or seemed obvious to me. I remember my older sister asking me how it all works and her disgust when I told her, "The man puts his thing inside you."

I recall touching my pussy with arousal as I watched Austin Powers and Alotta Fagina in the hot tub when I was four or five years old. In my preteen years, I'd stay up late and sneak into the living room to watch reruns of *The History of Sex* on The History Channel. I made sure to have the "previous channel" button preset to *SpongeBob* or some other inane children's show, just in case my dad came around the corner.

Sex was always taboo in my household, as was true intimacy and vulnerability. I didn't feel comfortable sharing my emotions or talking about my desires with my parents. As my body and the way men looked at me began to change in my preteen years, I felt embarrassed and somehow wrong, but also thrilled. I felt special and rewarded in my turn on. With no real guidance or mentorship, I decided to figure out *this sex stuff* on my own. This led to a lot of blind experimentation throughout my teens and early twenties. I courageously put myself in many potentially dangerous situations with men, who were usually a few years older than me but often had a decade or so on me. My unconscious intention was to explore, understand my desires, and find "prince charming." In the process, I experienced a lot of non-consensual sexual acts and violence, including rape and sexual assault. I didn't tell anyone. I blamed myself. For a long time, I felt like I needed to explain myself. To validate my wholeness. Even to apologize for my trauma. The thought of saying, "I've been sexually assaulted" filled me with a debilitating sense of fear. It made me feel damaged – unlovable even. In so many ways I made it my fault, as many survivors do. This story is not uncommon. I am not alone. It breaks my heart, but this pain became my purpose.

This is a foundational awareness in Tantra, that *both* can be true. We can both grieve the little one inside us who was abandoned, preyed upon, or forced to grow up before their time, while also finding peace (and, dare I say, purpose?) in the journey of reclamation.

It's not just those of us that were raped, verbally assaulted, trafficked, forced upon, groped, or otherwise that suffer. We are living an *epidemic of disconnection*. As a collective, we are completely ignorant of the sacredness of sexuality and the potential of intentional connection. *This is the path back home.*

My path began in my early twenties as the self-help and meditation industries boomed. I was totally on board with the affirmations, morning routines, positive thoughts, and daily yoga classes. But it only got me *so far*. I felt the instinctual pull deeper, into my darkness – **into my pussy**.

The summer between my junior and senior year of college, I had just come out of a four-year relationship and was miserable in every way. I had been slowly coming to the realization that the "American Dream" was less than dreamy. I had suffered and not addressed numerous experiences of non-consensual touch and rape. I had no idea what I really wanted to do with my life. And my body confused me. Luckily for me, I found a new lover who introduced me to Tantra. He wasn't a particularly special man. He certainly wasn't my normal type. He was short... older... average. But he had great style and *there was something magnetic about him*. I pulled the thread right into his bed and it **blew my mind.** It was the first time I felt so connected to someone while having sex AND I experienced my first penetrative orgasms. Previously, I could only climax from external clitoral stimulation. I hadn't quite figured out how to ride one out until then. The sex itself wasn't even that revolutionary. It was simple and loving. It involved more eye contact than I was used to and some breathing together. What stands out the most was the pure energy – the unspoken intention he brought to the table.

I would intuitively carry these foundations of Tantra into future couplings and started reading articles online every once in a while to learn new Tantra techniques. I read about using intention and breath to circulate energy in my body and with my partner. The first time I tried this with a boyfriend, I didn't tell him what I was doing, but I had my very first full-body orgasm. *It was bliss*. In those early days, I was really only into Tantra for the cool sex tricks I'd heard about from the neo-tantric lens. It wasn't until a couple years later that I began to research and understand the history, philosophy, and healing capabilities of Tantra, especially the more classic perspective. While sexual intimacy is associated more with Neo-Tantra, the philosophy of Classical Tantra has largely shaped my perspective and the contents of this book. For more on Classical Tantra, I recommend the work of Christopher Wallis, Sanskritist and author of *Tantra Illuminated: The Philosophy, History, and Practice of a Timeless Tradition*.

What really resonated with me about Tantra is the recognition that there is a physical world and a spiritual world, and there is an energy that connects them: sexual energy. The elusive and abundantly decorated world of Tantra is, in my opinion, for everyone. It is an invitation to create a holistic lifestyle that suits your deepest desires for soulful expression. By definition, Tantra incorporates many tools and modalities rooted in being present to encourage an expansive earthly experience. The word *Tantra* comes from Sanskrit, an ancient Indian language in which many religious and poetic works were scribed. The etymological root of the word (tan) means "to expand," while the suffix (tra) means "liberate." **Therefore, Tantra can be translated as an instrument for expansion and liberation.** Tantra is also often literally translated as "woven." In this way, we weave the moments and modalities of our lives for an expansive lifestyle of ascension.

The principles of Tantra have been utilized for thousands of years in various ritual, religious, and practical lifestyle contexts. There are countless lineages and approaches to the wisdom of Tantra, spiritual intimacy, and sacred sexuality, though many have similar principles and rituals. The tantric approach is simple, effective, and entirely holistic. Most healing modalities, philosophies of soul expansion, and religions leave out sexuality, whereas Tantra embraces this element of humanity as the most powerful energetic force in our bodies. Because of Tantra's full acceptance of this often taboo subject, many immediately associate Tantra solely with sexuality, when in reality, Tantra has so much more to offer.

Tantra invites us to be turned on by life itself. There are many tools in our tool box to refine our lifestyle and awaken this level of liberation and expansion. Sex is just one tool… but it can feel like the most accessible one to many of us. In the modern world, sex is often the only place we allow ourselves to really let loose and flow with our innate and primal desires. So starting in the bedroom is not a bad thing at all, but I promise you, the benefits of Tantra and sacred sexuality are sure to spill into every area of your life. *As above, so below.*

Within the various lineages of Tantra, including Hinduism, Shaivism, Taoism, Shamanic Tantra, Sacred Sex within Christianity, Egyptian Tantra, and Neo-Tantra, there are common **themes of presence, intention, and full integration of self.**

PRESENCE

When we see the present as our greatest gift, we are able to expand upon high frequencies of gratitude, peace, and bliss AND use low frequencies of fear, shame, and anger as opportunities to expand beyond patterns and limiting beliefs that no longer serve us. Being present means fully embracing our emotional state and recognizing that our outer world is a reflection of our inner world. When we tap into presence, there is an energy of acceptance and surrender. There are three tantric tools for tapping into the present and moving life force energy: breath, sound, and movement.

Breath encourages us to be present as each inhale and exhale can only happen in the moment of Now. It is innate and constant. Each inhale invites us to embrace what is, while each exhale invites us to let go of what is no longer serving us.

Sound is an incredible tool for moving energy (emotion = energy in motion). Incorporating sound, whether it's listening to rhythms or making our own sounds (sighs, moans, cries, screams, etc.), encourages us to move emotions instead of bottling them up, which is likely to cause disease in our bodies.

Movement is a celebration of our bodies, the earthly temple for our own divine. It is a gift for us to move in expression of who we are in the present moment. Moving our bodies also moves e-motion, in the same ways that sound and breath do.

INTENTION

Eros, kundalini, life force, feeling "turned on" – it's all the same and it is the most powerful energy known to humans. It is a force that literally creates life, our offspring. And yet this life force can do so much more. In many tantric and shamanic lineages, it is believed that each sexual act (including self-pleasure) results in a creative energetic exchange. This philosophy encourages tantric students to channel the surplus of erotic energy generated from pleasure into an intention aligned with their highest self. Intentions usually involve healing, invigorating our life, conserving our energy for purpose, manifesting deepest desires, letting go of what is no longer serving us, and/or capitalizing on our greatest potential for growth.

We learn to harness our sexual life force energy by being fully present and slowing down. Using meditations, rituals, yoga, and other modalities of tantric arts encourages conscious movement of life force energy, so one may begin to harness and direct the kundalini as desired.

INTEGRATION OF SELF

Tantra drops the judgment and encourages full acceptance of both our shadows and light. Without unconditional love and awareness of who we are, we block ourselves from the empowerment of choosing our highest self. Integrating our shadows means addressing deeply rooted limiting beliefs, shame, guilt and fear around sexuality and our bodies imposed by society and institutions. Shining light on your shadows empowers you to reclaim your eroticism.

When it comes to our shadows, Tantra encourages us to use intention.

Setting an intention allows us to look at the circumstances of our life objectively, then ask the question, "Does this align with my intention?" In this way, there is no right or wrong – there is only the wisdom of knowing if our thoughts, patterns, and actions are resonant with the state of expansion we deeply desire.

In Tantra, the individual takes responsibility for themselves, including their pleasure and their triggers. While we take personal responsibility and prioritize our relationship with ourselves, our external relationships act as an incredible tool to integrate our shadows. This includes our romantic, familial, professional, platonic, communal, and peripheral relationships. Our relationships are mirrors for our own experience. These mirrors show us the suppressed qualities of ourselves that we are not addressing. Within our most intimate relationships lies the opportunity to commit to a deeper level of expansion. When we show up in relationships, we energetically tell the universe, "I am willing to be vulnerable enough (*oh, the risk of potential heartbreak!*) to get to know my partner AND myself on a deeper level."

BEDROOM ARTS

Tantra encourages us to slow down and communicate our needs, preferences, and boundaries with our partners. Society has told us that sex always needs to be spontaneous; however, when we communicate these factors in an intentional way, we feel safe to fully surrender to sexual experiences. When we are able to set intentions as a couple for intimate moments, both partners are more likely to be in sync. Many tantric practitioners recommend prioritizing daily intimacy with both yourself and your partner. Intimacy does not always include sex. It could be physical, emotional, intellectual, or spiritual intimacy. And yet, when we open ourselves up to any kind of intimacy, we are more likely to desire sexual or sensual intimacy.

When sexual intimacy is on the table, there is a commitment to intention, often (but not always) slowing things down. Partners are encouraged to work through the lingering energy of their day to be fully present, letting go of any stress or tension with movement or meditation before joining as one. Breathe and relax together. Find yourself just being before initiating sex. Within the slow sex ritual, both partners abandon expectation and any "goal" of orgasm, especially peak orgasms (those that occur sharply and quickly, and usually end the sexual experience). This approach encourages valley orgasms, also known as edging (the practice of moving the erotic energy through the body, encouraging full-body, multiple, and longer-lasting orgasmic experiences). I recommend that tantric couples set aside four hours once a week for a longer tantric ritual. This doesn't mean having sex for four hours straight, but rather using this time to drop into your hearts, talk about your week, and slowly move towards sensual or sexual contact if it feels resonant for you both. Setting aside four hours means you don't need to rush into anything, so you and your partner can really listen to what your bodies and each other are truly desiring.

Singles are not left out of the tantric tradition and are encouraged to self-pleasure. This is a great way to increase self-intimacy and prepare for inevitable lovers to enter your life. Tantra teachings assert that the deeper one knows oneself, the greater their capacity to meet their partner in pleasure. So even in partnership, the individuals are encouraged to come home to themselves with masturbation.

In essence, Tantra is a path of "no rules" and all intention! BDSM can be tantric. The way you eat your food can be tantric. The way you hug, laugh, and cry can all be tantric. Bring the tantric perspective into any moment with the foundations of presence, intention, and full expression of self.

Over the years, I began adopting and exploring more and more aspects of living a tantric lifestyle. The more I leaned into the practice and philosophies, the more fun, abundant, and pleasurable life became. As I healed my relationship to my life force energy, my whole life changed. My sex didn't just get better; my relationships did too. My friendships were deeper. I started making more money. I got a new home and car. Work became more fun and in alignment with purpose. I healed my relationships with my parents. I was radiating. Happy. I was *turned on by life*. And people started to notice.

I had friends, family members, and clients come to me curious about what I was doing to find this joy and purpose. I excitedly shared what worked for me and it totally resonated with them. Despite all of the positive shifts in my life and resonance within my community, I still didn't feel qualified or "good enough" to become a Tantra teacher, coach, or bodyworker. It wasn't until one particular breakthrough with a dear friend that I finally awakened to my purpose of sharing this message with the masses...

One night, after a hot tub skinny dip, I offered to give Alexander* a massage. Alexander had originally hired me as a model for a hobby art project, but we became fast friends. He was a bit older and very successful in the tech industry. He was an immigrant who had one of those American-dream-come-true stories. Before that night, he had served as a bit of a mentor, having been such an inspiration for potential success, despite being the underdog.

We had spent a few hours earlier in the day taking photos for his new art gallery and then we had dinner. As we slipped into the hot tub, our light chat became more vulnerable. This depth in conversation had become more common for me as I dove into the world of Tantra. Individuals I barely knew would express how comfortable they felt around me and then would divulge secrets or ask me for advice. We broached topics of loss and love. Energy and emotions were flowing.

When we began to overheat from the hot tub, I suggested he lie down inside. After asking for consent, I began to incorporate spontaneous tantric bodywork. I massaged and connected with the energetic channel running from his perineum to the crown of his head, known in Tantra as the kundalini chakra system. With the heel of my left hand firmly planted on his root, I held his cock and balls, and with my other hand I held his heart. I told him I sensed a blockage in his heart chakra. The heart chakra is the home of the inner child and unconditional love. He began sobbing as he recounted being abandoned by his mom as a young boy. It was a glorious breakthrough in vulnerability from a man who was normally all business and emotionally avoidant. I held him as he moved the emotion (energy in motion) out of his body, creating space in his heart.

The next morning, Alexander messaged me in gratitude sharing the immense relief and expansion he felt from our impromptu tantric bodywork. He confessed that after decades of therapy, working with psychedelic practitioners, and other energy workers, he had never experienced anything like it. He then digitally sent me $1000 and said I deserved to be paid at the rate he paid his therapist for the results I created in our few hours together. Then he requested another "session" later in the month.

I spiraled. I don't do "sessions." What is he talking about? Was that sex work? Am I a sex worker? Wow, that's a lot of money. I don't deserve it. I have no formal training. I can't tell anyone about this. It was so easy! I'm so ashamed. But I'm good at it! Whatever "it" is… It was a one-time thing. I definitely won't do it again. Might as well enjoy the unexpected cash flow and go on with my life.

Despite the internal chatter, Alexander convinced me to join him in Tahoe for one night a few weeks later to enjoy the scenery and take a few photos for his new art gallery When I got there, he claimed he "forgot" his camera. We did another bodywork session. It was very different, yet equally powerful. The next morning, he coached me on my potential. He told me how much the world needed my gift. He told me he would refer all his friends and I'd be booked out as a tantric bodyworker immediately.

Of course he was the perfect person to tell me all of this. His own success was the product of seeing talent in unsuspecting places and building teams that literally changed how we approach the world. I trusted him. Something was coming alive within me. For the first time ever, I felt truly seen.

But I still couldn't really see myself. There were a lot of metaphorical cobwebs in the mirror. I had to look hard and long at why I was so afraid to commit to a path that had evidence of such healing and transformation.

CHAPTER 2:
COLLECTIVE SEXUAL TRAUMA

I was terrified to "come out" as a sex priestess. And I didn't for a full year, even though I saw the results, the healing, and the potential. I kept up some of my freelance writing and creative work while I secretly made most of my income offering Tantra massages and coaching on SeekingArrangement.com and SacredEros.com, an online Tantra directory. I waited five months to even tell my best friends. I wanted to be very sure about this new career path before I risked the potential heartbreak of being rejected by the women I loved and respected most. Thankfully, when I finally came out of the closet and explained my "why," they were wildly supportive. In fact, more than one of them responded with something along the lines of, "Of course you are a tantric priestess!"

To this day, not everyone is so understanding or celebratory of my gifts or even talking about sex. In fact, most people are downright awkward, demeaning, or judgmental, which just shows how much we're hurting as a collective in this area of our lives. In the modern world it is virtually impossible to grow up without some kind of sexual trauma, which can come from a variety of sources.

Even if you had incredibly evolved parents who offered a love and trust-based sex education with a bowl of condoms on the kitchen table, no one can entirely escape the media, especially TV and movies. I grew up in the age of *Degrassi*, *American Pie*, and *Cruel Intentions*, to give you some context. *Cruel Intentions* is STILL one of my favorite movies, yet now I consider how the film glamorizes shadowy sexual behaviors in a way that can be super damaging to impressionable minds.

Additionally, religion, school sex ed, and peers consistently project their own sexual shadow onto us. The Sexual Shadow are the qualities in ourselves we see as undesirable, and therefore do not fully accept or consciously work to integrate (more on this later). These fear-based ideologies are often so deeply rooted in our subconscious that we aren't aware we are allowing these limiting beliefs to rule our intimate lives. Not to mention the studies of epigenetics (more on this later) which show we carry the traumas of our ancestors, meaning even if WE didn't directly experience a traumatic event, such as sexual assault, our bodies may carry an imprint of those in our lineage who did. Translation: We might be unconsciously bringing someone else's trauma into our worldview.

And yet, it is with awareness that *we are empowered* to move beyond a victim mindset – to use these traumas as gateways into ourselves. **I say all this to empower you.** To show you where you may be limiting yourself unconsciously. The intention of these words is to *set you free*. You get to choose if the narratives of fear, limiting beliefs around sexuality, and judgmental stereotypes suit you. Or if there's something more expansive for your highest self – which, spoiler alert, there is.

Regardless, I can almost guarantee you received a lot of mixed messages from parents, religion, school sex ed, and especially pop culture and the media around what is deemed sexually acceptable. Most of these mediums are teemed with fear, shame, or guilt. Just as often, the media often employs the strategy "sex sells" to capitalize on our sexuality, completely disregarding expressed consent. Or they show intimacy only from a lens of primal passion with intense groping that borders on violence.

Media like this is nothing new – we grow up with it and are, in some ways, a product of it. My mom chose my first name from one of those hot romance novels from the eighties . It wasn't just her hair that was teased in those days. She clearly resonated with the main character, who is both vilified by her sexy figure and also seems to be in a constant sense of danger because of it. Nearly all of the sex scenes could be considered rape or bordering on such. This perpetuates dangerous messaging that our worth is directly tied to our ability to fuck, our bodies are dangerous, and rape is something to sensationalize. My mom chose my first name, which still lingers on government paperwork, because she identified with the book and the character. In my early twenties, alongside my spiritual awakening, I found it didn't resonate with me, so I took on my middle name, Leola. I adore it, I chose it – heck, it's on the cover of this book! It's my mom's middle name too and it means *lioness*.

But this book and its main character illustrate the divine dichotomy on our hands: Being sexy and having sex gets us fast and easy attention AND it is dangerous and wrong to be sexually liberated individuals. We may be deemed "trouble" or "dirty," often infusing derogatory terms such as "slut" and "whore" if we have the guts to reclaim our sexuality. We're damned if we do, and damned if we don't. One side tells us that to "be seen" we must sexualize and objectify ourselves, while the other says we'll go to hell for doing so. The modern woman is born with a Madonna-whore complex in her bones. Meanwhile, unhealed masculinity encourages the bros to greatly embellish sexual escapades to be seen as true man. *Ick*.

As we explored in the last chapter, the beautiful thing is that we're all sexual and *this energy is the fabric of our existence*. Cool, huh? Given that sexuality touches every part of our lives, literally, we can see how healing our relationship to our sexual selves leads to a whole new reality. And that is the true power of this work.

So sex brought me into this world, but I can confidently say that my parents weren't confident about sharing that fact with me. They surely weren't the parents with the bowl of condoms on the kitchen table, but they also didn't ignore sex entirely. They went with the "let's instill fear of the holies" angle. In other words, they informed me of the dangers of STDs and teen pregnancy and told me every boy was trying to get into my pants. I was severely lacking in any understanding of pleasure, my body, and the inherently spiritual nature of sex.

My sex education went a little something like this… I was always a bit mature for my age, so whenever my older sister Cara* was deemed old enough to know or do something, I was usually included. Even though she was a full two years my senior, I was grateful to have less of that older/younger sibling complex. We were treated fairly equally, as was our sex education. Our parents, who loved us both dearly, had divorced when we were quite young (I was 3 and Cara was 5). So when it came time to chat about the birds and bees, it was done in two different houses. I do have to say, hats off to my mom for attempting to educate us about our bodies with *The Body Book for Girls*, from the American Girl Library, which did go over the basics of puberty. But she went a little too far with her screening of *Kids*. This fiction film, released in 1995, is the scariest movie I've ever seen and is unfortunately based on very realistic events. It encapsulates every example of unhealed masculinity and immature femininity packaged in a coming-of-age tale, set in New York City in the early nineties.

When my mom popped this film into our VCR, I was in 4th grade, my sister in 6th. At the tender age of 10, I was far from ready for sex. And yet, the opening scene shows a 12-year-old girl (my sister's age!) being seduced by a 17-year-old. Full on penetration in the most uncompassionate way. My stomach is literally turned from the trauma of watching this film. As a young empath, I could immediately tap into the confusion of the young protagonist. At that point in my life, I had masturbated. I hadn't really known what I was doing, but I knew it felt good to touch my vagina. I had made the connection that sexual acts feel good, but I hadn't shared that intimacy with others. And yet, I truly identified with the confusion of this 12-year-old girl. I could see she really likes this boy and wants to please him by surrendering to the seduction. She also wants to give in to the beautiful, budding energy in her body, as we all do when we enter the altered state of consciousness known as arousal. But unfortunately, it is evident that we've really lost touch with the divinity of our eroticism, to the point that his energy is abused like a drug and this poor girl is completely taken advantage of.

She experiences no profound pleasure and is completely abandoned by her pursuer immediately following his release. As for the young man's perspective, I want to hate him, and maybe a part of me does. However, when I zoom out, it's evident that he isn't even aware of what he's doing or the more expansive options on the table. He's basing his experience off what he's observed and been taught by those around him, which likely went something along the lines of "virgins = good" and "having lots of sex makes you more of a man." To make the whole scene even more nauseating, following his release, he walks out of the room and disrespectfully spits on the family's living room furniture on his way to the door. At this point in the movie (which is just the opening scene), my 10-year-old self was so energetically and emotionally overwhelmed that I went to my room. My sister and mom finished the movie without me.

I went back and watched the film as an adult in the process of unpacking my own inherited sexual shadows. Suffice to say, the movie only becomes more tragic as it progresses, including depictions of sexually transmitted infections being contracted, drugs, pregnancy, and a grand finale of rape. It's obvious that my mother did all of this to protect me; we're all doing the best we can with the information and experiences we've been given. My mom was a teen when she had my sister. She wanted to halt the cycle – and she did! It came from love, but the intention was to instill fear. The intention was to traumatize us into abstinence. Isn't that wild?

Was your sex education traumatizing? Did your parents or educators use scare tactics or slut shaming to sway you from sexual exploration?

As mentioned, my parents are divorced, so my dad delivered the "talk" separately a couple years down the line… It was excruciating in an entirely different way. Pure embarrassment. When my dad and stepmom had us meet in my older sister's room, them standing at the foot of the bed, us sitting cross-legged on top, I literally thought we were being punished because of the amount of shame they carried in their bodies at the thought of having this conversation. When they opened the floor for our questions about sex, my thought was, *All the years I've lived, I've asked you questions about sex and my vagina and boy parts. And I've been told not to talk about this. And now suddenly, you want to talk about babies and how they're made? No, no, no, no, no, no, no, no, you've taught me to be ashamed of this. I'm not falling for your trick – we're not going there.* Suffice to say, I completely shut down.

And unfortunately, school wasn't really any better. I think the best way to describe my high school health class is from the scene in the popular film *Mean Girls* starring Lindsay Lohan. The sex educator, who is a man, says, "Don't have sex, because you will get pregnant and die! … At your age, you're going to have a lot of urges. You're going to want to take off your clothes and touch each other. But if you do touch each other, you *will* get chlamydia… and die." My experience was pretty much the same, although I did have female teachers. Maybe you relate?

JOURNAL PROMPT

How did you learn about sex?
Who taught you?
How did it prepare you or frame your perspective of sex?
Was your sex education intentionally instilling fear and shame?

In the case of religion, a lot of us have been told that God only approved of sex with one person, which is your spouse, so only after marriage, and it should only be used for procreation or as an expression of love. Wildly, there is no mention of using sex to have a deeper connection with God or spirit in most modern religions. This definitely wasn't addressed in my local non-denominational church. And yet, I didn't buy it. I found myself the most connected to something outside of myself at the brink of orgasm – here lay a thread to pull.

Upon further research as an adult healing my relationship to my sexuality, I found that pretty much every major religion talks about sacred sexuality at one point or another, including Christianity. *Oh the blasphemy!* But I'm not kidding. Sex is alchemy that brings new life into this world, via a direct connection to source. No wonder my orgasms feel out of this world. And no wonder religious authorities historically demonize many healthy expressions of sexuality; when we discover pleasure as a gift of empowerment and a direct connection to spirit, we become increasingly sovereign and embodied. This threatens the authority churches and ruling bodies have in our allegiance to them. **What better way to control people than by making them confused about the life force that brought them into this world and drives them throughout their adult lives?**

On top of a mostly (or entirely) fear-based sex education, we also carry the burden of past generations in our DNA. Consider the scientific fact that *a part of you existed in your grandmother's womb*. A female fetus develops all the eggs she will have in her lifetime while she is in her mother's womb – she will be born with all the eggs, which represent her potential for childbearing. This means you existed in your grandmother's womb as a teeny-tiny egg in your mother's baby ovaries decades ago. This is energetically significant, as your essence was present for any trauma your grandmother may have experienced while your mom was in her womb. And you were present in your mom's womb for the entirety of her life before you were born. Pretty crazy, huh?

If this feels a little to woo-woo for you, there are legitimate studies that prove we carry the trauma of our ancestors. This area of study called epigenetics considers how events in an individual's life may affect the way their DNA is expressed and passed down to their offspring. Epigenetics has found that the DNA code itself doesn't change, but it does flag potential adaptations in extreme or dynamic conditions. Epigenetics was first considered at the turn of the 19th century. It was observed that the sons and grandsons of survivors of US Civil War prison camps suffered higher rates of mortality than their peers, despite being well-cared for and having never directly experienced significant trauma of war. *Not surprisingly*, the fathers and grandfathers who survived the abhorrent conditions of the prison camps came home from the war with weak health and psychological implications that led to shorter life expectancy, but *it was surprising* their offspring suffered a similar mortal consequence. It could only be deduced the experience in the camps had somehow affected their gene expression.

Further studies on mice show more concrete evidence of generational trauma. In 2013, Brian Dias, at the time a researcher at the Yerkes National Primate Research Center at Emory University, began a study which exposed adult male mice to the scent of cherry blossoms, while simultaneously electrocuting their feet. He did this repeatedly until the mice began to associate the pain of electrocution with the scent of cherry blossoms. The mice were then bred with females to create the first generation of offspring. The baby mice were separated from their parents and raised by a control group of mice who had no experience with the electrocution or cherry blossom smell. When the babies matured, they were exposed to the scent of cherry blossoms. Those offspring who had parents triggered with the electrocution exhibited a stress response, while those who were fathered by the control group of mice had no response. The researchers allowed another generation to reproduce to create grandbabies of the traumatized mice, who also showed sensitivity to the cherry blossom scent. Brian Dias discovered chemical tags on the sperm DNA indicating gene encoding on the smell receptor. This proves the potential consequence traumatic events can create for an entire lineage of individuals.

Consider you could be unconsciously carrying the sexual trauma and rape of your ancestors. How would this affect your relationship to intimacy and sexuality?

While this might feel overwhelming for some of you to consider, it empowers us to *be the change*. Our generation gets to encode more expansive, abundant, and regulated gene codes for our lineages to come. When we heal our relationship to our sexual energy, find peace with our trauma, and discover the sacredness of sexuality, we are healing generations to come. We are creating unmarred potential for our children and our children's children, and onward infinitely.

It is my belief that all of this repression, misinformation, and shame is the root of most (if not all) sexual assault and rape. If we can replace this conditioning, if we can break the cycle and embrace our sexual selves with love and acceptance, sexual violence will massively decline and virtually disappear from our society. A study from the National Criminal Justice Reference Service found that offenders of sexual assault are ten times more likely to have been a victim themselves before committing their crime. I have also seen this pattern play out in my own life and in the lives of clients. Avoiding healing our relationship to our sexuality is dangerous to ourselves, the people we love, and the world. But the good news is that it is totally possible to heal.

While this book and myself, as the author, do not claim to hold the antidote to all trauma, nor can I undo the sexual violence you may have experienced, I can offer a perspective and set of tools to consider on your path to self-remembrance and wholeness. And *it all starts with getting really curious* about why you feel, think, and act the way you do. It takes the courage to look inside yourself – to consider the foundational beliefs you've adopted in life, which may be affecting your ability to experience true presence, receive pleasure, and create purposeful relationships.

HOMEPLAY
Sacred Sex Ed integration activities and expansive opportunities to transform the way you make love to life.

SEXUAL HISTORY TIMELINE
Supplies: pen and paper

1. With a piece of paper oriented horizontally, draw a horizontal line in the middle of the paper. On one end, mark your day of birth. The other end represents who you are today.

2. The middle portion is the duration of your life. Consider significant moments in your sexual history, such as:
- The first time you learned the biological differences of genitals and the characteristics of genders.
- The first time you learned the mechanics of sex.
- Your sex education from various sources.
- Your first experience self-pleasuring/masturbating.
- Your discovery of porn.
- Your first sexual experiences.
- Your favorite sexual experiences.
- Traumatic sexual experiences.
- Any celibate chapters (intentional or not).
- Any other significant moments in your intimate or sexual life.

3. Give each of the events above a notation at the correct time placement on the line.

4. Process internally as you go. It can be overwhelming or numbing to see all these events in one place. There is no right or wrong way to feel about your timeline. This is an exercise in self-reflection and acceptance. You may seek professional or friendly support from someone you feel safe with to discuss these things as they come up.

5. Objectively observe your relationship to the timeline. What did you learn or adopt consciously or unconsciously from the experiences on your timeline? What is missing from the timeline? What would you like to experience sexually? What would you like to learn or unlearn about your sexuality?

6. Consider extending the line with another piece of paper which represents your sexual future, including expereinces you would like to have with yourself or others.

CHAPTER 3:
AS ABOVE, SO BELOW

The way you approach your sexuality is likely how you approach the rest of your life. If you're rushed in your intimacy, you likely rush through your day. If you struggle to speak your fears or desires in the bedroom, you likely have poor boundaries or don't get what you really want out of life. If you don't take the time to make love to yourself on a daily basis, you likely struggle to have committed relationships that offer real depth.

There's an old adage that says, "How you do one thing is how you do everything," and one doesn't have to turn too many pages in any self-help book before they come across something along the lines of "As above, so below." It's happening in chapter 3 of this book! *Yay* – you made it. Happy to have you here. If you're a veteran of the self-help space, you know all about this, but we're going to go deeper into this philosophy, because most self-help books, philosophies, modalities, and spiritual lineages bypass the root of it all. While they may offer invaluable transformation, they are often ignorant of acknowledging sexual energy and how it plays into our healing and self-growth. They often stay where it's safe in love and light – ignoring all the glorious orgasmic potential in the fullness of the human experience. This is a huge disservice because, as we know from chapter 1, this sexual energy is literally the fabric of our existence. So, if we're skirting around sex, trying to be politically correct or avoid triggering people, we're likely leaving a lot of liberation and expansion on the table.

In Tantra, we say our outer world is a reflection of our inner world. Our inner world is composed of beliefs and thoughts that create stories and patterns, some of which we are conscious of, but most of which we unconsciously allow to control our ability to see the world in presence and neutrality. It is the human default to react to the world around us based on the stories in our subconscious, instead of being fully present to consciously take action based on our highest truth.

These stories and patterns operating in our subconscious or unconscious are often called shadows. Shadows can be distortions or golden beams of light. They are not good or bad. Our shadows do not make us right or wrong. But they can keep us from being our most expansive selves.

WHAT IS SHADOW WORK?

Shadow work is a term that we use in healing modalities and in psychology which relates to the working parts of ourselves that we deny or disown. This concept was coined by Swiss psychiatrist, Carl Jung. **He describes the shadow as the qualities in ourselves we see as undesirable, and therefore do not fully accept or consciously work to integrate.**

These beliefs and patterns linger in our subconscious and are often unconsciously projected into our lives, affecting our ability to maintain healthy relationships, take action in times of opportunity, and tackle our greatest obstacles in soul expansion.

The magic ingredient in bringing light to the shadows of our subconscious is simply the intention to bring awareness to our subconscious mind. **Self-awareness invites us to witness how deeply embedded trauma and conditioning shape our decision-making process and reactions.** With this awareness, we are able to expand beyond the limits of our subconscious to write our own narrative. Without this awareness, our inner world is often framed by inherited limiting beliefs and traumatic early experiences, leading us to make decisions not in alignment with our deepest desires or highest truth.

But what does this have to do with my sex life?

When it comes to intimacy and sexuality in the modern world, it is nearly impossible to grow up without some kind of sexual trauma, which we explored in the last chapter and will continue to illustrate throughout Part One of this book. As we learned in the last chapter, it is impossible to entirely escape the fear-based or hyper-eroticized narratives offered by entertainment, the media, religion, porn, school sex-ed, and our peers. These are often so deeply rooted in our subconscious that we aren't aware we are allowing these limiting perspectives to rule our intimate lives.

And yet, with awareness we are empowered to use limiting beliefs, triggers, and traumas as *gateways into ourselves*. Tantra asks us to integrate and bring unconditional love to all parts of our human expression, including our shadow. Doing so leads to more profound states of being. The deeper our self-awareness, the further we can expand outwardly – as above, so below. The greater your ability to fully feel and acknowledge your pain body, the greater your ability to receive pleasure, love, and peace.

For example, consider the potential of a new love. It takes true vulnerability to surrender to falling in love. Vulnerability may appear to be disempowering, but it's really expansive. **Vulnerability energetically tells the world you are willing to risk what feels "safe" in the name of change.** In the name of love. In the name of freedom – to open the door to new possibilities. To surrender into your deepest desires. When we fall in love, we are accepting the pain of inevitable loss. Whether the relationship ends with a breakup three months in or is until death do you part, the deeper and farther we go with commitment, the higher the stakes. Yet, without accepting this potential grief and heartbreak, we cannot experience the love and pleasure available in this new relationship. As we open the door to deep states of love, we are opening a portal of equal potential pain. As above, so below.

This mostly happens unconsciously, yet Tantra asks us to feel it all and bring it to the surface. When you proactively shine light on your shadows, you take full stock of how your traumas are keeping you in a state of fear and how your fears and limiting beliefs are hindering you from capitalizing on your greatest opportunities for growth. Shadow work empowers you to recognize how these traumas helped you grow or how these fears or limiting beliefs helped you survive, while also acknowledging that *the patterns that helped you survive are not always the same ones that will cause you to thrive.*

For example, you may have shut down your sexual self in your teenage years to survive high school and the wrath of your parents. It was a good call. You didn't suffer from gossiping peers or angry caregivers. But you also missed out on a lot of potential pleasure and life experiences. It helped you survive, but would you say you were thriving? **Now is the time to thrive.** It's time to let go of the fear of judgment and let yourself explore the wonderful world of sexual intimacy from an empowered, educated, and regulated place.

In this way, you learn to love each past iteration of yourself, including any perceived trauma or regrets. *You find peace in the realization that your shadow is what makes you a whole person.* It's what makes you relatable to someone. It's these characteristics that allow people to see themselves in you, and this inspires humanity to grow together.

Conscious co-creation is intimate. It takes vulnerability to bare your triggers, open up about your deepest desires, and share your intentions. The tantric perspective teaches the individual to take full responsibility for their pleasures and their triggers. We fear owning our pleasure and our fantasies because they are often demonized or taboo. Yet, sacred sexuality asserts there is no good or bad intention or desire – there is only the awareness of whether it is in alignment with your highest truth. However, a lot of our sexual behaviors are shrouded in elements of fear, shame, and guilt, limiting our ability to even become intimate with our authentic truth.

Do you feel let down by your sex life? Or do you feel like it controls you? Do you feel like there's got to be something more? There is. And it's in your shadows.

Sexual Shadow Work illuminates your limiting beliefs and deepest desires for presence, pleasure, and purposeful relating. It addresses deeply rooted limiting beliefs, shame, guilt, and fear around sexuality and our bodies imposed by society and institutions. Shining light in your shadows empowers you to reclaim your eroticism.

When we do not own our desires and our triggers, we often project them onto others. This may look like blaming your partner for not intuitively guiding you to peak orgasm, or judging another for their fantasies or preferences, or withholding love and affection out of fear of abandonment or assault.

So how do we bring light to our shadow? Doing so expands awareness of ourselves, while simultaneously bringing depth and truer love to our intimate containers.

4 WAYS TO INTEGRATE YOUR SEXUAL SHADOW WITH AWARENESS AND INTENTION

1. Observe your emotional reactions without judgment. Be curious about your triggers – they are usually direct projections of your shadow. When someone does something that causes an intense emotional response, see it as an opportunity to ask yourself why it bothers you SO much. Usually there is a part of you that fears the uninhibited expression someone else offers or you see an ounce of truth that threatens your own egoic beliefs. Your relationships are mirrors for what's going on in your shadows. **Example:** Your partner tells you they really want to try anal penetration. You are immediately disgusted and judgmental. Ask yourself why it bothers you so much that they want to try it. Is it *just* because you don't want to? Or is it because sodomy has long been chastised by religions and governments across the globe? Or is it because your mom said never to do that? Or maybe you were penetrated anally without your consent in the past? None of the above is wrong or "your fault" – but they may be limiting your ability to truly assess this desire neutrally. Take this as an opportunity to really see where this belief is coming from. This doesn't mean you are obligated to indulge your partner's desire. It is merely an invitation into self-awareness.

2. Be conscious of your internal dialogue. Does your inner critic or ego come out when you fantasize? Are you unconsciously judging yourself or others? Or letting opportunities pass you by because of limiting beliefs? Do you shut down before you allow yourself to explore the depths of the human experience? Usually this happens so quickly and stealthily in our subconscious that we don't even realize it. Set the intention to be more aware of your thoughts. **Example:** You see a Tantra festival in your area. You really want to go, but your internal dialogue immediately offers all the ways it feels impractical. *It's an unnecessary expense... I don't have the confidence... I'm afraid the teachings will change me and I won't recognize myself.* With awareness, you can use your internal dialogue to expand beyond these limiting beliefs. Quiet the critic by invoking your highest self, who may suggest taking on an extra shift to cover the expense, asking a friend to join you, and being open to change that facilitates deeper presence and growth.

3. Acknowledge your "light" qualities, while seeing the opposite in yourself as well. We live in a world of duality. To abandon one side of yourself is to abandon the fullness of your humanity. Let go of your ego and allow yourself to come home to the gift of a balanced soul expression. **Example:** If you see yourself as a giver in the bedroom, question your ability to receive. Are you using the label of "giving" as a way to avoid the vulnerability and surrender required to relax, let go, and receive? Maybe you struggle with fully receiving because your shadow says you must prove your worth by giving! You are inherently worthy of love and pleasure – owning this expansive belief leads to the embodied reaction of receiving with ease.

4. Embrace Sex Positivity. Encourage yourself to decide what it means to be sex positive and respect all others for their own expression of sex positivity. Create spaces to communicate and to admire others for their expression. Adopt the attitude of "Good for them, not for me" whenever you feel triggered by or judgmental of another's eroticism. **Example:** For you, sex positivity might mean pursuing a healing, committed, and monogamous partner and treating your genitals as a super exclusive temple. Meanwhile, maybe your friend has an explicit OnlyFans, making her rent by posting nudes, and is in a polyamorous relationship. You applaud her full expression of sexuality, while also honoring your own needs, preferences, and boundaries. You are able to celebrate and support her path to sexual liberation, while your path feels equally powerful yet manifests very differently. You remain open to your expression changing over time as you step into more alignment with your highest self.

So much of this process involves being conscious of our triggers. Triggers are experiences that bring us into a reactive state, often involving feelings of overwhelm, stress, anger, or confusion. *Triggers are there to keep us safe.* When something happens in your life that triggers you, the trigger is reminding you of what behaviors or patterns helped you survive the last time you experienced something similar. This is helpful in life-or-death situations but is not helpful when you're trying to heal trauma. *Triggers inherently keep us stuck in the past* because they trigger a re-action. We are reacting (re-acting), rather than being present and creating a reality that is a reflection of who we truly are and who we desire to become.

For example, your partner might trigger you by sharing their attraction to a stranger on the street. Rather than witnessing their beauty, you immediately find yourself in a dramatic spiral of comparison and fear of abandonment. Maybe you had a past partner cheat on you or break up with you and run off with another lover. Maybe you've been conditioned to believe we should only have eyes for our partners and anything else is sin. At the end of the day, there is nothing inherently wrong with wanting your partner to admire you above all else, but this state of reactivity is creating unnecessary stress for you and the partnership. What would it look like to get curious about what threat this actually has on your relationship, if any?

In this example, you'll see it is less about your partner being right or wrong to comment on another individual's appearance, and much more about *taking responsibility for your own reaction.* That person didn't trigger you. Your unresolved trauma triggered you. Their actions or behaviors reminded you of your trauma or limiting beliefs, which then triggered a fear-based emotional response which manifested as a reactionary pattern created to help you survive. It's time you take responsibility for your triggers. Putting the blame on someone else enables you to continue a pattern that leads you away from love.

I'm not saying to avoid communication with your partner, friend, co-worker, or whomever when something they do causes your unresolved trauma to rule your awareness. But let's move from "You triggered me" into "I'm feeling triggered by my past trauma. Can we hold space to talk about it?" In the example above, this may mean vulnerably sharing what comes up when your partner appreciates someone else's beauty. It may mean asking them to refrain from these comments until you feel more secure in your partnership (or indefinitely). It may mean asking for affirmation of their love and commitment or getting clarity on what their comments implicate. Are they simply just admiring another's beauty OR are they planting the seed for open-relating? **Using the trigger as a portal into greater awareness and dialogue creates space to evolve past your trauma and limiting beliefs.**

When we are triggered, our instinct is to go into a trauma response. This happens unconsciously, as your body interprets a potential threat and your nervous system and brain fire up, releasing stress hormones. There are four distinct ways we may react in the face of trauma or trigger: fight, flight, freeze, or fawn. Understanding these trauma responses, as well as which ones you tend to revert to, can be helpful in evoking presence and illuminating our shadows. When you are triggered and notice yourself going into fight, flight, freeze, or fawn, think of it as a flashing red stoplight. This is your invitation to slow down and get curious about what this response is telling you about a fear, stressor, or trauma.

When you recognize you are slipping into a reactionary state, this self-awareness invites you to shift into a more empowering place, come into the present, and heal past traumatic experiences. The way you respond to triggers may depend on the situation, but can also become chronic, especially with conflict in relationships.

> **Fight.** Responding to trauma by fighting is linked to the unconscious belief that *power and control* keep us safe and will lead to love or respect. When we think of this trauma response, our mind often goes to physically throwing punches, but it can also refer to verbal aggression, gossiping/rumors, punishing, or threatening. **Example:** You share a desire to connect sexually with your lover and they respond that they're not in the mood. You are triggered into feelings of unworthiness and rejection. You respond by pulling away from them entirely, punishing them for not giving you the affection you desire. They hurt you, so now you will hurt them.
>
> **Flight.** This response creates a tendency to *escape or avoid* pain, confrontation, or any form of distress. This can take a literal form of running away from a wild animal or staying long hours at work to avoid the inevitable confrontation with a spouse. It may also manifest as a sort of addictive personality, in which an individual uses a substance, hobby, work, alcohol, or otherwise to drown out the pain inside of them. **Example:** Your partner suggests you guys go to a couples sex therapist

to work on your relationship. Every time she does this, you change the subject or say you're too tired to talk about it. You continuously try to bypass the potentially vulnerable conversation to protect yourself from the pain of exploring your trauma and triggers.

Freeze. My go-to when triggered, the freeze response, causes the brain to *freeze action*, while remaining hypervigilant to threat of attack to determine when/if fighting or fleeing may offer a route to safety. This is a very common response to sexual assault. **All trauma responses are there to help us survive**. When it comes to being physically or sexually attacked, we may unconsciously believe it is safer to wait it out than to fight or flee, because taking action may make the aggressor even more angry and dangerous. If we freeze, we unconsciously believe we will survive the attack, which is priority number one, and deal with the consequences later. Freezing can become chronic and worn like a mask which entails hiding emotions, avoiding intimate relationships, and detaching from life. **Example:** Your partner is giving you a back massage. You feel him inching closer and closer to your ass. It feels way too much like that time years ago where you were non-consensually penetrated there. You start to go rigid. Your heart is beating faster and faster, but you don't say or do anything. You literally cannot think or process what is happening. You shut down and disassociate.

Fawn. Fawning involves *finding a path to safety* by placating the individual or situation threatening you. Having few or no personal boundaries, people-pleasing, and becoming a martyr are all forms of fawning. Fawning may lead to minimized abuse or conflict, but it often coincides with a disconnection from our authentic self. **Example:** In the middle of a sexual experience, your partner starts using degrading terms to describe you, such as "slut." You playfully go along with it... but it's kind of turning you off. Afterwards you feel a bit shameful and like you abandoned yourself for their benefit.

All of these trauma responses are instinctual and often get adopted and reinforced in our childhood. Being triggered is kind of like doing a *Freaky Friday* switcheroo with a much younger version of yourself. When we are triggered, we are immediately shifted into the consciousness in which we originally experienced a similar traumatic event.

For example, I once had an ex-boyfriend who would yell when we disagreed. It unconsciously reminded me of my parents yelling at me as a child. Back then, my parents didn't really want to hear "my side of the story," so I learned to fawn or freeze when they yelled. So whenever my ex started yelling, I'd revert to my inner 10-year-old and totally clam up. I'd usually eventually go into fawning, so it felt like I was always the one "coming back to love" and attempting to make up.

This relationship ended because I didn't feel safe to communicate my actual desires or express my true feelings. If I had recognized this pattern earlier, I could have acted much differently and potentially saved the relationship. While it would be easy and justifiable for me to blame my ex for fighting, I am just as responsible for enabling his behavior by continuously attempting to throw a Band-Aid over an explosive fight and my own turbulent feelings. It was the recognition of this pattern which allowed me to shift this reaction, so that in my future partnerships I was able to calmly communicate and rationally resolve disagreements.

This level of wizardry can take time, as we are working against thousands of years of evolution. According to Paul MacLean, American physician and neuroscientist famous for his research on the brain, there are three parts of the brain, known as a triune: the reptilian brain, limbic brain (mammalian), and the cerebral cortex. When we are exposed to an external stressor, it is the reptilian brain, the most ancient and primal part of the brain, which responds first via our central nervous system. Then the information of stress is processed by our limbic brain, where we give meaning to the stressor and react emotionally. We may be frozen there, or we may, finally, move our processing into the cerebral cortex. The cerebral cortex is where our higher levels of thinking come from – this is where we become consciously aware of our trauma response and consider whether a more evolved response is viable. So essentially, when we are exposed to a trauma or trigger, we can't help but respond first based on instinct and survival – *it's just how we're wired*. And our ability to move into critical thinking and conscious creation is dependent on our ability to regulate our nervous system to access higher levels of thought. Studies show that the most evolved part of the brain, the prefrontal cortex, is the most sensitive to negative effects of stress. Prolonged or collective trauma can severely limit

TRIUNE BRAIN THEORY

LIZARD BRAIN	MAMMAL BRAIN	HUMAN BRAIN
Brain stem and cerebelum	Limbic System	Neocortex
Fight or flight	Emotions, memories, habits	Language, abstract thought, imagination, consciousness
Autopilot	Decisions	Reasons, rationalizes

The Triune Brain in Evolution, Paul MacLean, 1960

our ability to think critically and evolve.

It literally takes evoking a more evolved part of ourselves to transcend our trauma response, heal, and have a more expansive response to challenging scenarios. Consider that you may reside permanently in one of these responses when it comes to your sexuality and/or relationship to your body. When we become aware of our patterned response, we are able to *let go of our victimhood* and *step into the role of conscious creator*. We reclaim our sovereignty. When you resolve your trauma, you stop taking things personally. When you take responsibility for your triggers, you begin to see them as opportunities to grow and become empowered. You're able to live in the present rather than in a reactionary state. *This is freedom.*

The processing I've described thus far has been all in the head. It has been awareness based, but it's also important to include the body when processing your triggers and trauma response. **You can't out-think what your body feels. You have to feel it to heal it.** Intellectually understanding what your trauma response is telling you is important for evolving and growing, but it's just as important to express the emotions arising so that we can truly be free from them. This is especially important for those that tend to veer towards the freeze and fawn responses.

It has been established that our most primal, animal brain responds first when triggered. What do animals do when they've just escaped a threat? Think about the gazelle who narrowly avoids becoming the lion's lunch. *She shakes it off.* She literally releases the emotion of fear by letting the energy (e-motion) move out of her limbs.

Take a note out of the gazelle's book by creating a sacred space to let the e-motion move. Utilize the three basic tools of Tantra: sound, breath, and movement. Have a tantrum, rage, cry, say the unsayable. Or dance, do yoga, go for a long walk, or simply jump up and down a few times. Experiment with what works for you to get emotionally clear.

The difference between you and this gazelle is that this gazelle will likely live with the potential of becoming prey for its entire life – it will be a constant stressor. Meanwhile, most of the factors that are triggering us are not actually threatening our survival or wellbeing in such a decided sense. Most of our triggers bear some resemblance to a past event but are not reflective of the true reality in the moment. Evoking awareness allows us to differentiate between what is actually a threat and what is an opportunity to grow, heal, or have a healthy conversation.

Upon discovery and awareness of our sexual shadow, we might be angry or judgmental of ourselves or the world for contributing to the pain, shame, or contraction it has created in our lives. This is normal and totally righteous. It is important to honor these feelings. Bypassing our rage only creates more shadow and distortion in our lives. I recommend finding an outlet for this rage using emotional freedom techniques, high intensity exercise, art therapy, emotional release, or a rage ritual (see below). On the other side of this anger or judgment, you will find an invitation for forgiveness, acceptance, and grace. We do our best until we know better and then we do better. Send past versions of yourself grace for keeping you alive to get to this place where you can now heal. Forgive your parents, teachers, and leaders, as they have done their best with the information they were given. And finally, we find acceptance in this world.

It can be hard to wrap our minds around the collective sexual trauma and violence in this world. It is critical we accept that *we are at an integral point in the evolution of our collective consciousness.* And as with any evolution or growth, there are growing pains. These growing pains often manifest as a light being shone into the darkest corners of humanity. We may be discouraged by what we find when we shine the light into the shadows of humanity, but in reality, this exposition is of the utmost importance to move forward with authenticity. Honor this timeline. *You can accept this as our reality while still holding space for a brighter and more equitable future for all.* In fact, it is the only way to hold ourselves accountable while creating a fertile environment for reclamation.

Applaud yourself for taking accountability for your sexual shadow. It can be incredibly complex and challenging to face these parts of ourselves. **There are depths of experience waiting to be discovered, as soon as you decide to do this "inner work."** It is a matter of the cost of inaction – this is not meant to scare you, but only to point out that doing this work is inevitable in order to live an expansive and abundant life.

HOMEPLAY
Sacred Sex Ed integration activities and expansive opportunities to transform the way you make love to life.

RAGE RITUAL
Supplies: pillow, journal/paper, and music

The intention of this ritual is to feel the anger, frustration, sadness, fear, and guilt of your sexual and relational past. This is a space to give yourself full permission to uncork the bottle of your consciousness and let her rip. You have to feel it to heal it. It may feel awkward, edgy, or even scary to lean in, but I promise you'll feel *so* liberated once you let go of the baggage you've been carrying.

1. Start by journaling 5-10 things that you find frustrating. Explore the range of simple pet peeves all the way up to the intricacies of human existence. Consider using your Sexual History Timeline from chapter 2 as a guide.

2. Then put on some loud, intense music. I prefer tribal sounds, but others enjoy angsty rock or ballads.

3. Give yourself space to surrender into a tantrum. Scream, stomp your feet, hit a pillow. Commit to a minimum of 10 minutes. Be careful of your surroundings, all the while.

4. Let the e-motion express itself and leave your body.

5. When you feel complete, scan through your awareness and ask yourself, "Is there anything else?" Ideally, keep asking until you feel the emotional charge dissipate and you come up blank. However, honor your body and the courage it takes to feel – do not push yourself if it becomes too overwhelming and you feel you need a break or space.

6. End by lying on your back and integrating with meditation or gentle music.

CHAPTER 4:

RECLAIMING YOUR POWER

You are so much more powerful than you believe. So much of this journey involves reclaiming the divine, badass, magical gift you are to the world. As you may have gathered from previous chapters (and from your own existence), it can be really fucking hard to remember who you are, or even to believe you have any amount of power or control over your life. And in truth, we can never have complete control. It is my belief that the universe is up to its own magic in gifting us the opportunity to remember ourselves by creating an illusion of oblivion. There is a beautiful flow birthed from falling in love with our unknowns, while finding trust in our own ability to adapt and create alongside the sometimes-unexpected whims of our personal universe.

In order to reclaim our power, it is helpful to understand where and how we have given it away. We've been conditioned to fear our own life force energy (our greatest source of power) and to look outside of ourselves for the answers. We live in a world where we glorify putting our trust in institutions that profit off our blind obedience. Namely, the state and the church have intentionally created fear to maintain a level of control. Both have historically created programs which demonize sexuality. Religion can be especially damning. Sex before marriage? *You're going to hell.* Want it in the butt? *The devil will have you.* Touch your clit just for funsies? *Hell. You must pay tithe (aka 10% of your income) to go to heaven – take your hand off your cock and get out your wallet if you want eternal life.*

When it comes to the government, widespread campaigns of fear around sexually transmitted infections, officials purporting their beliefs on marriage, and literal laws dictating our sex lives have led us away from exploring our divine, pro-creative energy. Did you know that herpes (genital or otherwise) was no big deal until the media realized they could profit off of selling newspapers plastered with headlines perpetuating a sexual epidemic?

In the height of the sexual revolution of the 1960s, scientists discovered a differentiation between HSV-1 (generally orally transmitted) and HSV-2 (generally sexually transmitted). Then, in 1976, *New York Times Magazine* published an article under the name "Viruses of Love" in which they benignly address herpes impartially as a "part of our individual and collective ecosystems—like bacteria and pollution. We cannot get rid of them without getting rid of ourselves."

But by the 1980s, the media was besotted with articles and advertisements purporting the rampant dangers of this virus. It was dubbed by *Time* as "The New Sexual Leprosy" in 1980 and then subsequently addressed by the same magazine as "The New Scarlet Letter" in 1982. Herpes made its official debut as the scapegoat of all that is "unholy" and "dangerous" in sex. This article, written by John Leo in 1982, claimed herpes was "changing courtship patterns, sending thousands of sufferers spinning into months of depression and self-exile and delivering a numbing blow to the one-night stand." These articles and countless others perpetuate a story of grotesque and pervasive stigma, despite only a modest rise of prevalence of herpes from 13.6 to 15.7 percent between 1970 and 1985, according to estimates published in the *American Journal of Epidemiology* in 2001. Additionally, for the vast majority of individuals, symptoms were relatively moderate, manageable, and infrequent (and in even more cases totally non-existent).

Why did the media change its tune?

It is suspicious that around the same time, pharmaceutical companies miraculously discovered and began selling several medications to "treat" herpes, when previously doctors had prescribed a simple bath. It is reasonable to assume that this whole smear campaign of herpes was a means to spread shame and rake in profits. Since the pharma industry is besties with politicians and politicians have the media moguls in their pockets (because cha-ching $$$), they all exchanged a bit of intel and money to make people feel unlovable and damaged if they have an outbreak. And *when people are in fear, they are distracted from their own power.* They are in survival mode.

This is not to say that the medications and information didn't potentially help millions of people (some of whom may be reading these words), but they also conveniently spurred a ton of fear and slut-shaming.

These days the Centers for Disease Control and Prevention (CDC) does not even recommend screening for herpes unless someone is actively showing symptoms – even if they have been in contact with someone who has tested positive! Due to the high rate of false positive tests and the risk of perceived shame and stigma associated with the virus, most doctors don't automatically include herpes tests in STI panels. It's also probably because in the worst-case scenario, your symptoms are red bumps or blisters similar to acne, razor burn, or a rash – hardly life-or-death. According to the CDC, approximately 11.9 percent of Americans between ages 14 and 49 have HSV-2 (the kind generally referred to as genital herpes), and most of them have no idea because of how infrequent and variable symptoms may manifest.

And yet, it's my experience that many adults would view this diagnosis as the end of their life as they know it. Even given all the facts presented above, I *still* hold fear of receiving a herpes diagnosis and having to communicate it to potential partners... not so much because of the symptoms, but because of how I may be perceived by others in a vulnerable setting. I have never been tested, as I've never had symptoms. Given my sexual history, there's definitely a considerable chance I fall into the nearly 12 percent of adults in my age range who are positive for genital herpes, but given the CDC's guidelines, I'm not a candidate to be tested.

There are other more direct ways the government may restrict our sexual expression. For example, there is a legitimate and active law in Texas that prohibits citizens from owning more than six sex toys (as of 2024). Section 43.23 of the Texas penal code states: "A person commits an offense if, knowing its content and character, he wholesale promotes or possesses with intent to wholesale promote any obscene material or obscene device... A person who possesses six or more obscene devices or identical or similar obscene articles is presumed to possess them with intent to promote the same."

Fingers crossed the attorney general of Texas doesn't get his hands on this book... *just kidding.* I hope he does – even if this ends in my imprisonment for owning seven dildos. Censorship may be considered an elevated form of flattery if I contemplate the company I keep. Historically, some of our greatest healers, scientists, and thought leaders, such as Jesus, witches, Joan of Arc, and Galileo, were publicly persecuted for going against the grain and following their truth, bliss, and/or intuition.

But why would the church and state be SO invested in our sex lives?

Well, what better way to control people than by making them afraid of the very energy which created them? The very energy that has the power to liberate and heal people, allowing them to unconditionally love themselves and others. It is a political strategy and it has worked for thousands of years. Consider the Council of Nicaea, 325 AD. Called forth by Roman emperor Constantine, the intention of this Council was to bring together leaders of the church from all corners of the sprawling empire to come to a consensus around religion. This sounds well-intentioned, but in reality it led to much persecution, as "God" rightfully means something different for each of us. Yet, anyone who publicly shared a truth that was not in congruence with the official doctrine of the organized church was met with persecution and, most often, death. This religious despotism, supported by the states, *enforces a sense of conformity that draws people away from the divine within themselves* and leads to corruption and manipulation of power by those in authority.

This is just ONE well-documented and widespread event in history – consider the innumerable other more localized or privatized events. One more story, which is more personal to me, is the denunciation of Mary Magdalene. She who was Jesus's equal and known as the Apostle of Apostles was rewritten in history as one possessed by demons – a common whore. In reality, I have no problem if Magdalene actually was involved in sex work, and in some ways, I believe this claim to be true (see chapter 15 for more on what it means to be a holy whore). However, Pope Gregory I, in 591 AD, used this claim to intentionally discredit her and perpetuate a precedent of demonizing feminine leaders. He stated, "We believe that this woman [Mary Magdalene] is Luke's female sinner, the woman John calls Mary, and that Mary from whom Mark says seven demons were cast out...

to perfume her flesh in forbidden acts." It is clear that women had been purported as a lesser sex far before Mary Magdalene, but her story feels especially significant to me, as I was raised in a traditional Christian community, in which the vast power of the feminine and intuitive wisdom were minimized. Studying Magdalene brought me back to my Christian roots in a holistic and gloriously empowering way. If her story is calling you, I recommend exploring the following books as resources for inspiration: *The Magdalen Manuscript* by Judi Sion and Tom Kenyon and *Mary Magdalene Revealed* by Meggan Watterson.

In saying all of this, I want to be clear that I don't believe government, religion, capitalism, or even the patriarchy is inherently "bad." I truly believe that each of these institutions brought massive growth to humanity and our collective consciousness. I also don't believe these sources always consciously desired to instill fear and disempower us – I believe that in just as many cases our leaders and authority figures were doing the best with what they had, based on the knowledge, beliefs, and trauma they inherited. And yet, there gets to be balance. These institutions encourage the values of intellect, critical thinking, intelligence, and science. I love all these resources and use them liberally in my daily life. Yet, we equally need feminine wisdom, namely intuition, honoring nature, and reclaiming bodily autonomy.

The macrocosm is a reflection of the microcosm. Our abandonment of the feminine is pervasive and exemplified abundantly in our material world. It is no coincidence that one in three women report direct experience with violence or assault, according to the World Health Organization. It is no coincidence that our waters and land of Mother Nature are in the shape they're in due to mass pollution and toxins. It is no coincidence that up to one third of mothers report birth trauma (PATTCH). We've been collectively ignoring women, missing out on the gifts of their oracular wisdom, and, in the process, failing to protect them. Masculine forms of intelligence call for us to look outside of ourselves for the answers – to look to the government, science, and authority. Feminine wisdom asks us to feel, to go inward, to connect with our body for the answers. When we integrate the feminine and masculine perspectives, we become limitless.

I also want to be clear that I am referring to the *energies* of the masculine and the feminine. Many of our best scientists, religious authorities, and government officials are women. As a woman, I still identify with masculine qualities of ambition, responsibility, and space holding. I'm *good* at being masculine. Many women are, not just because we are rewarded for fitting into this mold society has given us, but because we all *have both*. Men and masculine identifying individuals have an equal opportunity to connect to feminine energy and wisdom. Being a man doesn't make you a better authority figure or better at science, and being a woman doesn't make you inherently more intuitive and nurturing. It is my belief that we all can benefit from evoking both masculine and feminine perspectives in our day-to-day lives.

But the truth of it is that as a society we've been putting a lot of emphasis on the masculine way of running things. Having the courage to listen to your body and experiences, rather than relying solely on external influence, is rebellious in the best kind of way. It means saying the uncomfortable thing when it's easier to stay quiet, advocating for your pleasure and needs, and questioning every societal expectation or conditioning you've ever received. This takes a lot of courage – for all genders. Women have largely been conditioned for generations to be agreeable. They have been taught to abandon themselves again and again. It's also hard for men, who have been taught that feeling is a weakness and to solve problems with violence. And it's hard for everyone in between on the gender spectrum – I can't imagine nor can I speak from any direct experience about what it is like to have the world impose their beliefs on these core pieces of identity.

Yet, when we lean into this discomfort and trust ourselves, it is SO worth it. I wouldn't be here writing this book without following my intuition, which guided me towards investing in experiences, mentors, and resources that my brain said I couldn't afford, my schedule said I didn't have time for, and society told me were "weird." I wouldn't have a multi-6-figure business, the relationship of my dreams, or the uplifting community I love and cherish. *Listening to your intuition is one of the highest forms of self-love and a divine rebellion in the same token.*

You are your own healer. You are your greatest teacher. Don't look outside yourself for the guru or the leader. Of course there is much to be learned from those who have walked the path before you, from our loved ones, and even from our societal institutions, but I suggest taking everything with a grain of salt – *including this book and my words!* Maybe there have already been things you've read here that haven't landed, that you've disagreed with, or that have downright triggered you. If so, I'm sending all the respect your way for continuing to read on with curiosity. I have not had a single teacher, coaching container, book, or self-development program that I have believed or resonated with whole-heartedly, but I also got at least something – one takeaway – from each resource I've sought out. This comes down to what I've dubbed the trinity of higher truth. When considering external influence, I suggest evoking these three concepts: respect, discernment, and sovereignty.

THE TRINITY OF HIGHER TRUTH

Respect. We feel respected when there is regard for our feelings, wishes, rights, or traditions. Consider, do you feel respected by this source, whether it be a person, pamphlet, or politician? If not, move forward with increased caution or consider aborting the influence entirely.

Discernment. We use the quality of discernment to decide what is contributing meaningfully to us and what is not. Be very curious about the motivations of the source. Be open-minded, but use your judgment and trust yourself. Ask questions – lots of them!

Sovereignty. We evoke sovereignty as conscious creators of our reality. At the end of the day, you are responsible for yourself. You get to set boundaries and ask for what you need to feel safe to receive support or take influence. Use your voice, take space, and take care of yourself above all.

As much as I preach being your own healer, teacher, and guru, I sure have hired tons of them. I also have a shelf full of self-development books, listen to podcasts on the daily, and am constantly referring those in my network to opportunities, resources, and containers I believe could help them. Taking guidance from those who are a couple steps ahead can feel like you have a cheat code, it can increase accountability, and it can be so much fun – *we don't have to do it alone!* Work with others, but trust your own intuition above all else. If someone makes your spidey senses go off, get curious about it! But also remember to consider the potential that your fears, limiting beliefs, and unconscious patterns can disguise themselves as your intuition.

Now that you are fully aware of all the places you may have been led away from your power, you get to truly reclaim it! This is simply done by no longer giving your energy to the false stories perpetuated by these sources or your subconscious. It won't happen overnight, and it will likely last a lifetime. Think of it as a delightful game of hide-and-seek. As you learn to trust yourself more and more (which we'll illustrate in the next chapter), you will naturally become increasingly aware of where you've given your power away. And you will be more inspired to do you. You reclaim your power by letting go of the false stories and choosing to show up as your full authentic self by doing what you love and trusting the rest to follow.

You aren't here to slurp society soup and live the "American Dream." You are here for YOUR dream. Your purpose. To share your love and to feel absolutely juicy while you do it. This is much easier to do when you're surrounded by a like-minded community. So much of our power goes out the window when we do things for the love, approval, or attention of others. So make a commitment to **do it from love – not for love.**

Doing it from love means you aren't acting out of the desire to receive love as a reward or validation. Ironically, "doing it for love" is literally a survival mechanism. We inherently want to be accepted, loved, and chosen by the group, because if we aren't accepted by the group or by another, it could mean death. In ancient times, being cast out by society made you susceptible to predators and enemy clans. Our bodies haven't forgotten this. And I truly believe we need community to thrive. But you know what also gets in the way of thriving? Abandoning our authentic self. And doing things FOR love often means abandoning ourselves in the process. It often means we're operating from scarcity – afraid that if we fall out of favor, we won't be loved.

When we do things FROM love, we feel safe to be our full selves. We set heart-centered boundaries, we become more playful, and we call each other forth. We know that the more we love ourselves, the better a match we are for the highest love available: unconditional love.

Unconditional love is about giving freely and unconditionally, without attaching strings or expectations. Trust that the more you dismantle false truths and allow your authentic self to shine, the more magnetic you are to attract soul-aligned community.

HOMEPLAY

Sacred Sex Ed integration activities and expansive opportunities to transform the way you make love to life.

MIRROR MASTURBATION RITUAL

Supplies: mirror, blankets, and lube/personal massage oil

If I had a dollar for every time some guru or life coach or self-help book told me to take a good hard look at myself in the mirror to get all the answers, I'd be a millionaire. And what do you know, they were onto something.

If you are in the market to fully love yourself, in shadows and light, there is no more direct route than by looking at yourself in the eye (and genitalia) whilst you make love to yourself. Mirror masturbation fosters self-confidence, body acceptance, and empowers you to take ownership of your pleasure. It allows you to soul gaze with your flawed, human self and your inner divinity simultaneously.

1. Stand in front of a mirror, fully clothed to start.

2. Begin by simply eye-gazing with yourself – looking into your own eyes for a prolonged period. This may be as far as you go the first time – that is okay!

3. Try taking off one piece of clothing at a time until you are naked in front of the mirror. Pause here for more eye-gazing.

4. Say kind words to yourself, both about your body and who you are as a person. What are you good at? What do you like about yourself? Say it to yourself, as if you were a lover.

5. Slowly begin to incorporate self-touch and massage. Start with non-erotic touch and don't rush to the genitals.

6. If you're feeling aligned and alive, incorporate your genitals. Make love to yourself. Witness your body change with pleasure.

CHAPTER 5:
TRUST YOURSELF

You can only reclaim your sexual self as deeply as you trust yourself. As we've learned in previous chapters, we've inherited and created lots of stories around our sexuality. Many of them probably feel pretty limiting, and yet we've held on to these stories because we didn't know any better or because there was a sense of safety in staying within the lines. However, this is the journey of becoming a conscious creator – your own guru and leader. It is time to create your own truth about your sexual self and expression. One must listen to their intuition to truly capitalize on all that life has to offer them, *in and out of the bedroom.*

Let's clear this up by getting clear on what intuition actually means. Intuition is the link between your current self and your higher self. Intuition is often associated with the third eye chakra, the space just above your brows, in the center of your forehead. The third eye chakra enables us to trust ourselves – to tap into an inner knowing that transcends our five material senses. It is our ability to sense beyond what is physically perceptible or measurable. A balanced third eye chakra is wise, intuitive, and self-empowering. When the third eye chakra is in alignment, the individual is able to balance the outer, fact-based world with their own inner trust and intuition. One trusts themselves, their body, and their experiences.

This is also where the pineal gland lives. Traditional science says the pineal gland's primary function is to regulate your body's sleep and wakefulness cycle by secreting melatonin, a hormone that signals drowsiness. In the spiritual communities, it is believed the pineal gland is significant to communicating with the universe and unlocking our awareness as spiritual beings. René Descartes, famous French philosopher, called the pineal gland "the seat of the soul." Powerful stuff. *If you believe in it.*

I once coached a woman in my *Sacred Intimacy* program who said the idea of having a portal in her forehead (third eye) actually scared her. *Could some demon or entity get in there? I don't want people to think I'm crazy...* This may be some of that ancestral trauma coming up after centuries of witch hunts in which women were literally burned at the stake for following their intuition.

For thousands of years, we've been conditioned to fear everything to do with witches, from black cats to Friday the 13th. In reality, these women were healing people, honoring nature, and trusting themselves above the authorities of the time. But, as we've gathered, empowered individuals are a threat to powers held by institutions and, therefore, must be condemned and prosecuted swiftly and publicly, sending a message to any others who may be considering veering outside of the socially accepted and narrow narrative of the day.

Did you know that Friday the 13th used to be a day to celebrate the divine feminine? The number 13 is associated with femininity, as there are 13 moon cycles in a year... and female menstrual cycles naturally sync with the cycles of the moon. So the number 13 represents the beautiful gift of procreative ability and the cyclical nature of women. The word *Friday* comes from Freya, the Norse Goddess of love, beauty, fertility, and sex. Her equivalent in Latin languages and cultures is Venus. The French word for *Friday* is *Vendredi. Venus... Vendredi...* Do you see what I'm getting at? In ancient times, each day of the week was devoted to a divine being, and Fridays were all about love, femininity, and sex! So Friday the 13th was traditionally the day of the Goddess – not at all in alignment with the propaganda of the horror industry. Of course, this reconditioning happened over thousands of years, as patriarchy and capitalistic influence dominated.

In my opinion, it is no coincidence that the governing bodies would desire to steer individuals away from any movement which encouraged people to look within for answers. If people are looking within, then they aren't looking to these institutions which profit off of their fear-based leadership. *Now is the time to come back to our bodies and back to love.* There is no greater act of self-love than listening to your intuition. Your intuition honors your experience, your body, and, most importantly, your highest self. Our conditioning of martyrdom can make following our intuition or self-love out to be selfish. I disagree. *When you prioritize yourself, you prioritize everyone else.* When you fill your cup all juicy and overflowing, you show up in the world as your whole, yummy self. The world needs more well-nourished and authentic babes. So when you take care of yourself first, you're doing our planet a big ol' favor.

How do you start tuning in to your intuition? You get out of your mind and into your body.

GETTING OUT OF YOUR HEAD AND INTO YOUR BODY

At one point, I decided to stop asking the universe for signs. I decided to ask my body instead. I gave her the power. I allowed my body to lead my desire and resistance. To honor her choice. Now I see there is a universe inside me. I know what is for me and what is alive inside me. *My body is my mystery school.* And now I invite you to find your universe within. You know your body, experiences, and needs better than anyone – why look outside yourself for your answers?

That being said, as we learned in the last chapter, we also very much get in our own way. All of us have voices in our head of fear, self-doubt, and sabotage. For a lot of us, these voices shout at us and drown out the subtleties of our intuition. Our trauma, limiting beliefs, and fears keep us stuck in reactive and harmfully instinctive patterns of victimhood and disempowerment. These survival patterns may be disguising themselves as your intuition. Let's get clear – **instinct is not the same as intuition.**

We've all heard the adage "Trust your gut." *Is your "gut feeling" the same as your intuition?* Yes. And no. Sometimes. Oftentimes your gut is actually your instinct. Intuition and instinct are two distinctly feminine forms of wisdom. Intuition is the link between your current self and your higher self. Intuition communicates through a certain sense of "knowing" information in alignment with your highest truth. These usually show up as flutterings in my upper chakras. They may also be experienced as a "light bulb moment" – those moments where an idea or truth seems to fall from the heavens into your head. Our intuition may also be communicated with visions, signs, or other extra-sensory happenings. These extra-sensory happenings (seeing, hearing, knowing, or feeling things that can't be explained by the material realms) are deeply shamanic and also greatly misunderstood. Fear or mistrust of those who are extra sensitive to the spiritual realms may be another product of manufactured fear and distrust of the divine feminine and embodied wisdom. For me, when I get an intuitive nudge, there is often a sense of neutrality (at least until I've judged the intuitive hit as good or bad) – there is a clear absence of fear, and usually an obvious presence of love.

Instinct, on the other hand, is *geared towards your survival*. It communicates experiences you've known (i.e. past trauma) or information that has been carried in your DNA via your ancestral line (i.e. epigenetics). These usually show up for me as "gut feelings" or butterflies/stomach turnings. There is often a sense of density and groundedness to my instinctual hits. Both intuition *and* instinct can be very powerful allies in growth and healing. They are also both primal, innately accessible within us. Often they are in resonance with one another. Sometimes they are not. Gut feelings and instinct are primarily there to keep you safe, which is super important, especially in situations with legitimate danger ahead. But *instinct can be limiting*, especially in circumstances where it is safe to push your edges to create opportunity for expansion. The actions and mindset that help us survive are not the same ones that help us thrive. We often mistake our instinct for our intuition. This could be holding you in fear-based patterns and conditionings that no longer serve you. My suggestion: ask the "nudge" or "hit" where it's coming from. Feel into the sensations in your body and take note what part of you feels activated.

For example, when my fiancé (now husband) asked me to move into his one-bedroom apartment until we found a house to buy, I was immediately a "no." **Instinctually** I became contracted at the thought of living in tighter quarters. Not being able to host clients, meaning I'd have to scale back my work, taking the dog down 23 floors to use the bathroom… I felt like my whole life would become harder and so much less "me." I told him this repeatedly, but he wouldn't let it go and eventually it led to a breakdown. I was pissed. I felt like he wasn't respecting my needs or boundaries.

And then my higher self gave me a sign: *"What you seek is seeking you."* **Liberated.** That's how I felt when I saw this quote posted on a wooden sign at a wellness resort on the way to the bathroom after my kundalini class in Tulum, where I was working on a private retreat with a client. I hadn't been able to focus or truly drop in during the entire flow as my mind was spiraling in relational drama. Andrew and I were going through it. I'd like to say he was being a total asshole and not hearing me, but in reality, he was seeing and hearing me better than myself. That's how it goes in divine partnership – your person is your mirror. They show you what you can't see. And thankfully Andrew is *really* committed to being that mirror for me, persistently waving the truth in my face until it finally clicked.

In that moment, my **intuition** kicked in and I realized… I wanted to do less and be more. And Andrew could help me, but it would take letting go of the steering wheel for a second and letting him drive. I realized I was being a control freak. *I needed things my way to feel safe.* I was operating out of fear. Out of instinct. The last time I moved in with a partner, it kind of blew up in my face – not to mention the chaos of my youth as a child of divorced parents. Constantly bouncing back and forth between Mom's house and Dad's house. Having stability in my home is very important to me to thrive and keep a regulated nervous system. I realized I was totally purging my childhood and past-relational trauma all over our relationship.

It was keeping us from moving forward, and it was keeping me from what I really wanted: support and permission to follow my joy. I had also recently been feeling an intuitive nudge that I should restructure my business – scaling back many of my core one-on-one offerings to create space for group containers that reached more people and truly lit me up. When I read, "What you seek is seeking you," I had a "light bulb moment" of clarity. I realized that the argument between me and Andrew was a reflection of me getting in the way of what I deeply desired. He wanted to support me, and I was stuck in a survival pattern of taking care of myself. In the busyness of hustling to provide and survive, I didn't feel I had the time or stability to restructure my business – that would have meant slowing things down. I had instinctually become hyper-independent and control was my safety net. But what I actually wanted deep down was less control. Someone to trust. To co-create with. What I really needed was someone to support me as I reconsidered how to live my purpose. Moving into Andrew's tiny apartment for a couple months could mean working less and doing more of what I actually loved. It would also mean less stress of finding a new place in the interim and moving all my things. When I had that "aha" moment, I realized I don't have to do it alone. I can trust this man. And most importantly, I trust my surrender.

When I shared my realization with Andrew, he softened. In the end, we decided to prioritize finding a larger place to live in, but one Andrew could afford on his salary alone. This way, as my business transitioned, I'd have a security blanket, just in case. We ended up not needing the extra financial security, as I was able to pivot my business into much more impact, joy, and ease while maintaining my level of income. But it's so much easier to follow our intuition when we feel safe and regulated. If I hadn't softened into Andrew's suggestion and found a middle ground, I may still be playing small in my work, reaching fewer people and feeling less inspired.

In many ways this truth was liberating, but it also deeply challenged my inner feminist. Trusting yourself and your intuition doesn't always "make sense" at first. When I began opening my third eye, miracles and saving graces became my reality. I narrowly avoided dangers by odd twists of fate. I heard voices and music that others didn't. I sensed energies that others had no capability to comprehend. And I was TERRIFIED to tell people what was happening to me. So I didn't. It wasn't until I became embodied and created love and safety in my being that I truly began to trust myself and share my intuition with others.

Listening to both your instinct and your intuition requires you to listen to your body. Being embodied means listening to your body and trusting its wisdom. This can be difficult as we've collectively rejected the body, especially in its nakedness. Most bodies are deemed completely unacceptable, as they do not match the stereotypical, socially acceptable standards, leading to much shame and self-hatred. The nude body is often highly sexualized. But the truth of the matter is that **the naked body is a gift**, used to experience the world and each other. This body has climbed mountains and plunged into seas. It has danced until sunrise and shook with laughter countless times. This body has fallen down and picked itself back up again. This body has made love and defied expectations. This body is a tool and a treasure to be cherished. When we heal our relationship to our body, in all of its nakedness, we are more likely to trust the signals it sends us. Nudity is not inherently sexual. Naked bodies are not sexual by definition, nor are they wrong or offensive. Nakedness shows strength and beauty. Nude art is rarely created for the purpose of sexual pleasure – it is the viewer who sexualizes a nude image.

At the same time, this sexualization goes without judgment because sexuality is normal and beautiful. When we understand it and are able to channel this energy in a healthy way, we are able to use sexuality as a tool for enlightenment. Without shame and free of fear, sexual thoughts and acts are a celebration of love, life, oneness, and creation. When we heal our relationship to our sexuality, we are more empowered to distinguish between aligned *turn on* and instinctive *arousal*.

This starts with ourselves – treating our own bodies as sacred. We become intentional in how we use our bodies to explore the depths of the human experience and pleasure. We get clear on our desires and boundaries by listening to her (i.e. intuition), and then respect them by communicating clearly what we need and want. We speak kindly to our bodies. We take care of ourselves. We are able to intuit the types of food, exercise, relationships, media, and otherwise that are supporting our wellness. We prioritize holistic well-being. We accept our bodies and our sex.

Take time to figure out what you like by literally making love to yourself with a yoni or lingam massage. Approach your genitals with curiosity, as if you were experiencing your body for the first time or as if you were exploring a new lover's body. Invest your time and resources to expand your orgasmic potential – read the books, listen to the podcast, work with a sex coach, tantrika, or therapist! Train yourself to be with the shifts in your energy. Does your body feel open and receptive in a particular environment or around certain people, and then closed in others? Why is that? What is your body trying to communicate to you? This is your intuition at play!

Following your intuition is an act of devotion. It is one of the most powerful ways to treat your body like a temple. Yoni is the Sanskrit word for vagina. It directly translates to "temple" or "holy space." We often take for granted the portal that brings life into this world. A gateway between the spirit world and Earth exists between each woman's thighs. Even if they are not actively gestating and birthing a human child, it is clear the creative capacity of vulva-owning individuals and others who identify with the yoni (including trans and intersex individuals). Wouldn't it be beautiful to truly honor this sacred space? With each interaction with ourselves and with our lovers, whispering prayers and adoration as we do in the grandest cathedrals, mosques, and temples. Instead, we are too busy demonizing its sacred blood and expecting it to have the eternal youth of a bare pubic mound.

Penises, on the other hand, are harshly judged for their size, their circumcision or lack thereof, and/or their straightness. Lingam is the Sanskrit word for penis. The lingam is associated with the God Shiva and penetrating consciousness. The Shiva Lingam is akin to God. Your cock is God. Their cock is God. *Praise be and get on your knees.* Kneeling before God just became a whole lot sexier.

When we treat our bodies and our genitals as sacred, we begin to see all they do as sacred. We integrate our sexual centers with our spiritual centers (i.e. our highest self). We respect ourselves and treat ourselves with love and care. We let go of the judgment on our bodies.

As you shine the light on your shadows and heal from sexual trauma and conditionings, it can be easy to judge past versions of ourselves and carry resentment towards individuals and institutions that enable further collective sexual trauma. I, for instance, used to carry a lot of regret and self-judgment for not speaking up about an experience of sexual assault when it happened. I didn't report him, nor did I share what happened with my friends or family for years. I have also carried shame for cheating on a lover. I held on to anger towards my elders, religion, and educators for their demonization of sexuality and failure to educate me properly in regard to safer sex. All of these feelings, while totally valid, weighed me down and kept me in a cycle of victimhood.

Reclaiming our power also means dropping judgment of ourselves and others. Every time you carry judgment for yourself, you are giving your power away. Every bit of resentment towards yourself, the elders, and societal systems fuels their power. *How long will you let them live rent-free in your head?* This is why grace, forgiveness, and gratitude are so important on this journey. Grace, forgiveness, and gratitude empower us. These qualities shift us from victim to conscious creator of our reality.

We do our best until we know better, and then we do better. We get to give ourselves, and all past iterations of ourselves, grace, knowing we did our best in that moment, in that season of life. You literally didn't know any better. You were following the script you were given OR you let your instincts take the lead, which may have caused you to react by fight, flight, fawn, or freeze. Now you get to rewrite the script. Now you get to do better. Forgive yourself for ever judging yourself for your pleasure, preferences, or patterns of reaction. Forgive yourself for letting your fear and shame control you for so long and for believing any narrative of shame or any judgment imposed by the people in your life and by society. Send them love and forgiveness, as well, knowing that our parents, teachers, and leaders are doing the best with the information they've been given.

Simultaneously, set an intention in your heart to change the narrative. To halt the passing down of these limiting beliefs of fear, shame, and guilt. Choose trust and resolve to create spaces for authentic expression within your own self-pleasure and with partners.

Embodied grace, forgiveness, and gratitude is an act of reclaiming your energy.

HOMEPLAY
Sacred Sex Ed integration activities and expansive opportunities to transform the way you make love to life.

FORGIVENESS RITUAL
Supplies: pen and paper

As part one comes to a close and to get the most value out of parts two and three of *Sacred Sex Ed,* it is recommended to let go of judgment, resentment, and shame. This process will help you do so.

1. Write a letter of forgiveness. You will likely feel called to forgive more than one person, including yourself, your parents, religion, your teachers, peers, past sexual partners, violators, etc. Address lingering resentment and be honest with yourself about who you feel ready to forgive. Consider if you believe certain individuals do not deserve forgiveness. I do not recommend you push yourself to write a forgiveness letter, unless you can truly do it with compassion, grace, and authenticity. You may not be ready to forgive everyone who has wronged you, crossed your boundaries, given you false information, or otherwise. That is okay.

2. You may need to do several rage rituals (see chapter 3) before you have felt it all and feel ready to release the charge. Your forgiveness letter may look something like this: *I forgive myself for not saying no. I forgive myself for listening and taking my parents' sexual education to heart.*

I forgive my ex for forcing me to have sex before I was ready. I forgive Amy for making fun of the way my pussy looks. I forgive myself for pressuring my husband to try new things in bed. Etc.

3. Consider lighting a candle and burning this letter over a deep pan or fire-safe bowl. Otherwise tear it up into many small pieces to symbolize the alchemy of release.

PART 2

Expand Your Awareness

CHAPTER 6:

INTENTIONAL INTIMACY

There is no right or wrong – there is only intention. How liberating to adopt this perspective? Being intentional is a pillar of Tantra and sacred intimacy. So much of our life is goal-oriented. We tend to base our worth on results, value, and what we produce. We have sex for the orgasm. We work for the money. We do the thing to look good. It's all about doing.

Goals are about doing. *Intentions are about being.* Intentions allow us to co-create with the universe from a place of non-attachment and curiosity. When setting intentions, we are encouraged to consider *what is available in the moment of now?* Releasing attachment to an outcome or goal creates liberation. When we are focused on a sole outcome, such as orgasm, we may miss all the other magic available on the journey. Just like water running from a faucet, the more we try to "grab" the goal, the more it evades us and the less we enjoy the gorgeous sensation of *flow*. Intention invites presence and trust.

So much of my life, I operated very unintentionally. In some places I followed what everyone else was doing, and in others I completely rebelled just to spite the system. Sometimes it felt like I was throwing spaghetti at the wall to see what would stick. I tried on lots of new kinks and lovers and crazy outfits. I wasn't doing anything *wrong*, but I was often going in circles and repeating patterns, rather than expanding into my higher self. For example, in my late teens and early twenties, I became very involved in the kink world. I watched a lot of BDSM and public degradation porn. I signed up for *Seeking Arrangement* and *FetLife* (websites for non-traditional relating). I would have sex with people I met on these sites, and I would masturbate to those genres of porn. I always felt shame after. I would orgasm and then a wave of grief and guilt would wash through my body. I didn't understand it and I didn't want to. It hurt.

When I began my sexual healing journey and started doing shadow work, things began to shift. I turned my energy inwards and slowed it *all the way down*. I became very energetic and sensual and, in some ways, vanilla in the bedroom. I cracked open. I was so sensitive that partaking in the kinky, BDSM world became untenable. When I watched the porn I used to like, I would end up crying and feeling sick to my stomach. Tuning into my journey at that time, it's clear the darker edges of sexuality were not serving me. That doesn't make BDSM, fetish, and kink *bad* or *wrong*. But based on my intention to come home to myself and heal, they weren't in alignment (more on this in chapter 14).

In fact, with further introspection, I realized I was historically gravitating towards these themes as a way to re-live my sexual trauma; as a way to get control of past experiences in which I was abused or manipulated. I was going in circles around my trauma. I took a couple years to intentionally distance myself from these themes in my sexuality. I processed my non-consensual sexual experiences and assault. I met myself with tenderness and love. I set new standards (which we'll explore in the following chapters) for my lovers and invoked empowering practices to communicate my desires and boundaries. I created safety, softness, and presence by focusing on my relationship to self first, and then using tools of Tantra and safer sex with partners.

From this grounded place, I began to explore sexuality all over again. I became playful and curious. I saw my eroticism as innocent and sex as sacred play. I slowly pushed my edges of sex-ploration until I found myself back in the realms of BDSM and kink with clear intention. From a healed place, I experienced these darker and more primal realms of sexuality as a way to explore the depths of the human experiences; as an opportunity for sacred surrender (more on this in part 3). In BDSM, I found an opportunity for pure presence. An invitation to let go and receive with the intention of vulnerability. A catalyst to expansive states of being, soul evolution, and profound freedom. What was once *all wrong* became *alright*. The difference was intention.

When it comes to our shadows, Tantra encourages us to use intention. Setting an intention allows us to look at the circumstances of our life objectively, to then ask the question, *"Does this align with my intention?"* In this way, there is no *right* or *wrong* way – there is only the wisdom of knowing if our thoughts, patterns, and actions are resonant with the state of expansion that we deeply desire. When it comes to setting intention, I like to think of it as a way of being, which brings us closer to the North Star of our higher self. **Everyone benefits when you're the most you.** You become more you as you liberate from what's no longer serving you and step into expansion. We explored how to liberate yourself in part 1 of this book – now we are getting into the expansion bit.

When setting goals, most of us look for evidence of what is possible by considering what has been done in the past, what we've seen others accomplish, what we feel we are worthy of, or what feels possible. We claim or call in what *makes sense*. When setting intentions, **instead of focusing on what we have evidence for, consider what feels most expansive and liberating.** Allow yourself to want what you want without putting limitations or judgments on what is possible for you. Acknowledge your authentic desires – not the desires that have been watered down or filtered by your conditioning. Consider your individuality; consider what a bigger and better life means FOR YOU.

I once had a lover who said, "What are we calling in?" Every time he touched my pussy, he asked me this question. Depending on what was alive for us individually and as a pair, we would call in *peace, community, ease, wealth, joy, surrender,* and a potentially infinite number of expressions of being. In many tantric lineages, it is believed that each sexual act (including self-pleasure) is a creative energetic exchange. Eros, kundalini, life force – it's all the same and it is the most powerful energy known to humans. It is a force that literally creates life, our offspring. And yet this life force can do so much more. This philosophy encourages individuals to set an intention to direct the resulting surplus of erotic energy. Intentions usually involve invigorating our life, conserving our energy for purpose, manifesting deepest desires, addressing biggest challenges, and capitalizing on the greatest potential for growth and/or healing (see more in chapter 12).

Pairing intention with our most powerful and sacred energy is the best kept secret in creating a life you love.

Evoking intention is also incredibly powerful in identifying patterns and triggers that no longer serve us. Doing so empowers us to expand beyond our current faculties into those of our higher selves. Simply deciding to be curious about our internal dialogue encourages us to take radical responsibility for the status of life we are creating. We then get to be intentional about thinking, speaking, and acting in greater alignment with our highest possibilities.

Sexual liberation can look many different ways. To some it looks like being chaste, and to others it looks like celebrating wildly and erotically. To me it's all about intention. Are you covering up out of fear of being sexualized, of being labeled slutty if you don't? Or is it because keeping your intimacy to yourself feels most sacred?

Alternatively, are you publicly sharing your eroticism for the ego? For fear of commitment? For attention? Or to celebrate and share your abundance of life force and self-love? To inspire and awaken others to their sacred sexuality? There is no right or wrong way you express your sexuality. It's all about the intention. Is your expression in line with the expansion that you deeply crave? In this case, the outcome looks different for each person and can evolve greatly over a lifetime.

How exciting is that? That your preferences and boundaries can expand and contract as your intention becomes more aligned with your highest truth.

As you embark on your healing journey in reclaiming your sexuality, you may feel called into a "hoe phase." The much-esteemed Urban Dictionary defines a "hoe phase" as follows:

A phase in your life that occurs frequently when you are fine with exploring promiscuous activities and connecting with random people. These activities do not always end in sex, but they can lead to it. You have a high tendency to dance provocatively with strangers, be a tease in social settings, flirt non-stop, kiss and/or make-out with others, and get caught up in the moment. This phase helps you establish what you like and don't, explore your sexuality, and have fun. You have the ability to stop these actions or snap out of the phase.

A hoe phase can be very healthy when pursued intentionally. I certainly had my own phase (or 4) with varying degrees of conscious intention.

If you're feeling called to explore your eroticism in abundance, it's important to consider two things:

> Intention. What is your why for abundantly sharing your eroticism? My favorite intention for a hoe phase is to honor the divine magnetism I feel with another, trusting there are cosmic lessons with each person I share that chemistry. I also desire to share my perspective of sacred sex with many, which is done very effectively by actually introducing them to my sex. And I love using slut phases to focus on my own healing/self-love, while still getting my needs for intimacy met. Yet, it is important to be aware of shadowy desires for external validation, fear of deep commitment, and lack of self-worth. These can often sneakily co-exist alongside our more expansive intentions. Always be curious and self-aware to integrate your shadow (see part 1 of this book).

> Safety and consent. It is still important to respect yourself and others throughout your hoe phase, which means consciously communicating your intentions and sexual health status. This empowers your partners to authentically consider what they're available for. We'll explore these topics more intimately in chapters 9, 10, and 11 of this book.

For some, the hoe phase is more than just a phase – it's a legitimate lifestyle. One conscious form of sluttery is polyamory (meaning many-loves), which we will explore more in chapter 10. Within the vast umbrella of polyamory, there exists a niche relating structure known as *solo-polyamory*. Solo-polyamory means you are your own primary partner, while also creating space for external love and relationships of depth to blossom. Being solo-poly doesn't necessarily mean you have many sexual partners. It's more about being open to many loves with a primary commitment to yourself.

I've had many a hoe phase and one intentional season of solo-polyamory the year before I got engaged to my life partner. When I decided to consciously take on the label of solo-poly, I had just gotten out of a year-long relationship with a man I thought I'd spend the rest of my life with. As that relationship blew up in my face, I realized there was a big gap in my understanding of what I wanted in a deep, committed partnership. I was also really hurting from both the loss of that relationship and the grief of releasing our shared vision.

Solo-poly was perfect for me because it allowed me to get my needs for physical, emotional, and sexual intimacy met, while I focused on my healing and explored my true priorities for a committed relationship. It lasted a glorious five months before I decided I was ready to find the man of my dreams. He sauntered into my life two weeks later. I have friends (and past lovers) who have taken on the label of solo-poly as their indefinite relating style. While solo-poly served me for a mere season of life, others find this relating style to be the most liberating and expansive for them in the long term. Talk about a reclamation of sovereignty and sluttiness!

At the end of the day, no matter what form it takes, your inner slut deserves love. Your slut IS love giving itself freely. *Because love is limitless, she doesn't want to play small in how she expresses it.*

I spent most of my life questioning whether my full range of sexuality was lovable. Years of conditioning and societal trauma of slut-shaming gnawed at me like an irritating parasite. I worried men would not commit to me because of how generously I overflow into the world. Because of how easy it is for me to see the best in others and want to love all of them for it. Many men wanted to own my love. I worried women would ostracize me. Blame me for loving their men too openly. I feared they'd feel threatened by the fullness of my expression.

At the end of the day, I let that shit go in favor of spreading the love and the gospel of sacred sexuality. However, healing our sexuality doesn't always need to look like a broadcast to the masses. It could also be the exact opposite (or something in the middle!). Many feel called to the opposite of sacred sluttery, known as *conscious celibacy.*

For years I was highly skeptical towards the concept of conscious celibacy. I witnessed this trend running through the spiritual community and my spidey senses went on high alert. I perceived it as another way to impose shame and limiting beliefs on intimacy and sex. It felt like the collective was trading one set of religious restrictions for an upgraded set stamped with the guru's approval. *NO, NO, THANK YOU, NO.*

But then, during the first full moon after I declared to the universe I was ready to manifest and commit to my life partner, *Spirit* asked me to be celibate for a full 28 days. I was very resistant at first, but as I let my ego take the back seat, I intuitively knew harnessing my energy inward was in my highest good. That was the official end of my solo-poly season. And three days later I fell in love with Andrew, my husband. Inevitably, we didn't have penetrative sex for the first five weeks of our relationship. The energy between us was equally overwhelmingly tempting, yet also so powerful it deserved the reverence of divine timing and spaciousness. We explored in other ways and I upheld my commitment of celibacy for the entire moon cycle. Thankfully, Andrew was incredibly supportive and totally on the same page. We knew we had the rest of our lives to have sex and quite enjoyed the purposeful pacing of our erotic expression. As we slowly unveiled our sexual selves to each other, everything felt so new! In the past I would see, touch, and consume a man's cock all within the first few dates. With Andrew, we went on many dates before I was even allowed to see it! Then it was several dates later when I was allowed to touch. Each of these milestones became great moments of reverence and devotion as we invited and initiated each other deeper into our physical temples.

What is celibacy? Simply put, celibacy is the practice of abstaining from sex. However, sex can be defined in many ways and is a bit subjective. Some people refer to celibacy as completely closing off from any form of sexual AND much physical intimacy (including holding hands or hugging). Others may define celibacy as only refraining from a certain type of sexual activity such as penetrative sex, leaving space for booby gropes and hands in the pants (anything but penis-in-vagina). Some even rationalize anal sex as a workaround for those desiring penetration but wanting to maintain chaste.

My resistance to conscious celibacy came from my mistrust of religion and authorities of my past (such as sex educators and my parents) who preached abstinence as the holy way. At this point I have proven that sex *can be* just as sacred with yourself, as it is with a new lover on vacation, or with your life partner. Again, it comes back to intention and your openness to treat it as such. While I do believe there are countless individuals who use celibacy in a high-vibe way, I'd wager there are just as many operating from fear.

School sex educators teach abstinence as a way to avoid the "life-ending" conditions of pregnancy and STDs. Many religious authorities promise an eternal afterlife in heaven under the condition that we abstain until marriage. Which sounds *oh-so-beautiful* (and I'm sure it is for lots of folks), but I've worked with countless others who were severely let down on their wedding night – and for years to come. And yet, I truly believe even in these cases there can be some karmic *happily-ever-after*. My real gripe with the focus on abstinence is the insinuation that chastity is synonymous with purity, while sex is synonymous with dirtiness.

In 7th grade, my physical education teacher stuck six inches of clear packing tape on Sarah Smith's forearm. She ripped it off and then she stuck it on Rachel Elm who stuck it on Ashley McNair and on down the line until I received a piece of tape covered with my peers' fuzzy hairs, skin cells, and oils. This was meant to demonstrate the filthiness of one's nethers after slutting around... or even "losing" your virginity to someone who had numerous partners. I also abhor the concept of "losing" virginity (what about *gaining* a beautiful, intimate experience?!), but I'll save that battle for another day.

I thought once I healed my relationship to my religious indoctrination, education system, and fear-based approach from the parentals, I'd be rid of this purity madness. Think again. This mindset is exasperated by the spiritual communities who preach sex as a:

S: SACRED   E: ENERGY   X: EXCHANGE

Which, I actually agree with. What I can't get behind is the fear-inducing proclamation that we will be cursed by the energy of our ex or that one-night stand for years to come... or until we have a shaman wave sage bundles over our wombs. Many spiritual teachers claim that because sex is a sacred energy exchange, when we connect sexually with another, we take on their energy, trauma, and vibes (especially the bad ones). I am pro-sage bundle, but this logic totally undermines our power and autonomy as sovereign creatures of God/spirit/the universe! It is the same chastity message wrapped in shinier paper.

Some not-so-expansive reasons to choose celibacy include fear of intimacy, desire to be perceived as a "good girl/boy," life altering repercussions (which are easily avoidable or figure-out-able), going to hell, being judged for sexual expression, the wrath of authority figures, or being perceived by your guru as impure. That being said, when celibacy isn't being approached out of fear, it can be downright liberating and expansive.

If you're feeling called to explore conscious celibacy, it's important to consider two things:

Intention. I love the intention of using conscious celibacy as a way to focus on oneself and to reevaluate our relationship to sexual connection. We expand by going deep within our own internal landscape without the distraction of others. Yet, it is important to beware of shadowy desires for external validation, fear of wrath, and purity constructs. These can often sneakily co-exist alongside our more expansive intentions. Always be curious and self-aware to integrate your shadow (see part 1).

Indulge in other sources of pleasure. Try tantric yoga or breathwork. Nourish your body with delicious foods and elixirs. Dance! Make art! Find other ways to channel this energy towards self-love and radiating divine love.

Great beauty, sacredness, and reverence may be found at both ends of this sexually expressive spectrum and at every place in-between. Give yourself permission to tap into your intention and consider in which ways your sexual self will feel most primed for evolution into your higher self. Full permission to change your mind at any moment!

HOMEPLAY
Sacred Sex Ed integration activities and expansive opportunities to transform the way you make love to life.

HIGHER SELF MEDITATION
Supplies: peace, quiet, and music (optional)

This exercise is meant to help you connect to and clarify your intentions for more expansive and liberating intimacy.

1. Put on some gentle meditation music or step outside into the organic sounds of nature.

2. Consider using a guided meditation to connect you to your higher self. One can be found on the *Talk Tantra to Me* Podcast episode 46: https://www.talktantratome.com/podcast

3. After relaxing your body and dropping in, call forth the energy of your higher self. Your higher self can be perceived as a future, more healed, and/or evolved version of yourself. It is you on a higher timeline.

4. Consider, how do they perceive their sexuality? How do they express it? What relating structure and preference do they embody? Is this in alignment with how you currently approach intimacy? If not, what's the gap? And what can you do today to begin closing the gap?

5. Allow any messages to come through from your highest self without expectation or judgment. Be curious about where your mind flows in this time, paying special attention to feelings, visualizations, sensations, thoughts, words, symbols, or otherwise that may flow into your consciousness.

6. End your meditation by setting an intention to use this clarity to choose a relating style that supports your current season of expansion.

CHAPTER 7:
TYPES OF SEX

Before my invocation as a pleasure priestess, I thought there were two types of sex: good sex and bad sex. Lo and behold, looking back, most of my sex was "bad" sex, in that my bar for "good" sex was very low – I wasn't asking for what I really wanted, I was fuzzy on my boundaries, and, mostly, I didn't even know what was possible. I had only an inkling of the transformational and restorative capacities of intimacy. I was blindly leaving the potential of deep emotional connection, healing, and orgasmic bliss on the table. I left the quality of my sex up to chance, as I went in with zero intention and expected my partners to read my mind about what I liked.

It's no wonder, given that I certainly didn't receive any sacred sexual education from my parents, the church, or in school, and the boys I connected with were even more clueless than me, in most cases. I intuitively knew there was something more for me in the bedroom, which led to a glorious slut phase or two. During said "phases," I gave myself a wide berth for exploration. I traveled the world and experienced love making across cultures. I signed up for social networks for sexual and kink exploration. I went to Tantra workshops. And my relationship to my sexuality slowly began to transform; I began to transform. I healed my relationship to my body, my pussy, and my orgasmic potential. I educated myself, like you are doing now! Heck, I'm still finding new depths to explore in my body and in the bedroom, and I hope I never stop finding new ways to meet myself and my lovers.

As time has gone on, I've become much more intentional about the kind of pleasure I'd like to facilitate with myself and my partners. Over time, my intimacy has naturally become more emotionally connective, pleasurable, and transformational. I didn't have a particular framework or language to describe it until I attended an ISTA training (International School of Temple Arts). Their teachings of Shamanic Sexuality identify four types of sex: reproductive, recreational, restorative, and transformational.

Reproductive sex is exactly what it sounds like. It is sex with the intention of making a baby. It is my experience that reproductive sex is the most acceptable across the world. There are many religious institutions that claim reproduction should be the *only* motivation for sex.

Recreational sex has the intention of enjoying bodily pleasure and passing the time. And that's about it. Just for fun, for the orgasms. It is my experience that this is the intention for most sexual behavior. This kind of sex could be described as just "getting off" and the goal is often to have an orgasm sooner rather than later (or never). Nothing wrong with that, but there's a lot more available when we consider the energy we're working with. As we've learned in previous chapters, our sexual energy is our most powerful creative force; when we reclaim that power and heal our relationship to it, we create potential for healing, liberating sexual experiences, and expansive orgasmic potential.

Restorative sex is using intimacy and life force energy to heal the body, mind, heart, or soul. Restorative sex feels so empowering, knowing you always have access to this energy inside you which you can channel to heal yourself. Restorative sex can manifest in many different ways and can heal innumerable parts of ourselves, but it all comes down to energy and emotion. Many of us don't feel safe to express our emotions and often avoid them, minimize them, or bottle them up. Stifling energy in motion creates dis-ease in the energetic body. When we don't express our e-motions, it may manifest as a physical/mental disease or malaise. When you have restorative sex, intentionally or not, you are actively moving energy. You are inviting e-motion to release, clear, and heal. For this reason, restorative sex can be very cathartic; it can bring up past traumas; it can feel like therapy. Remember from chapter 1 of this book, sound, breath, and movement are the three Tantra tools for moving stuck e-motion and dropping into presence. When we have embodied sex, we organically incorporate all three of these tools at the same time! Full circle moment.

Transformational sex offers the divine experience of changing your life, the way you see the world, or the ways you connect with others. It is my experience that transformational sex feels like a plant medicine journey, whether I am self-pleasuring or with a partner. It feels like I've transcended my individuality and I feel the oneness of the universe. Transformational sex can lead to cosmic orgasms – those in which you feel like you've left your body. It could also mean exploring new things in bed, like kink or new positions, or connecting with more than one other person or energy. These sorts of sex-plorations can reveal new and transformative paths to pleasure and presence, shifting the way you perceive yourself and the world.

At the end of the day, it's my belief that there is no right or wrong intention for sex or intimacy, as long as it's consensual for everyone involved. Yet my work involves educating individuals on the range they're capable of. Most people operate solely within the realms of reproductive and recreational sex. Often they've accidently had restorative or transformational sex, but don't have the words for it and believe it was just chemistry, luck, or fate, not realizing their power to be the conscious creator of their sex life.

Another powerful thing to recognize is that not all sex cleanly fits into just one of the four types listed above – they often overlap. For example, sex that is purely reproductive feels a bit *ick* for me. The thought of having sex only to procreate makes me feel like livestock. I want love and magic when I'm baby-making! I desire pleasure and empowerment and transcendence, whilst consciously conceiving. I would say most individuals conceiving aren't having purely reproductive sex – it at least becomes recreational, as well.

And a lot of us are having healing or transformative sex without even knowing it or without having the words to describe it. For example, have you ever had make-up sex? Or sex after a fight? When my partner and I start to bicker with each other, we actually consider, *When was the last time we had sex?* Often in those cases, it's been more than a few days since we last connected intimately with depth and intention. As a solution, we prioritize time for intimacy – we come back to love. Having sex when you're angry or upset works because sex has the capacity to move energy, especially when done in a tantric fashion. Sex awakens our life force, which can be channeled up our energetic system, clearing, cleaning, and releasing "stuck" energy and e-motional blocks. We can use sex, especially very primal sex, as a way to move low-vibration energies out of the body. We can use sex, especially loving and connective sex, to deepen intimacy with our partners and welcome in high-vibration energies of peace and gratitude into the body and relationship. Sex is an incredible tool to have in the conflict resolution tool box within relationships, as long as you're also using your words to communicate your intentions and being realistic about what both partners desire out of the connection.

Some couples may be using sex as a Band-Aid for serious issues in a relationship, such as lack of true compatibility or enabling of toxic or abusive behaviors. Remember – pleasure is an altered state of consciousness; therefore, just like any mind-altering substance, it can cause us to think irrationally or succumb to unhealthy patterns of co-dependence and addiction to the relationship. So within the realm of "make-up" sex, get really clear on the current state of affairs and be honest with yourself and each other about any underlying challenges or opportunities for growth in the partnership. While sex can be very powerful for connection and intimacy, it is not a panacea for relationship woes.

I have definitely used the excuse of really amazing and transformational sex as a reason to stay in toxic relationships, and I've guided countless clients in recognizing the same thing. What we don't realize is *it's usually us* bringing the magic, transformation, and healing to the sex and relationship. We are capable of all of it on our own OR with a new and more compatible partner.

I once held space for a client as she went through a breakup. She shared she wasn't just grieving losing this man, she was also grieving the amazing sex they had. He was the first one to "make her" squirt like a sprinkler *every time* they connected. I reminded her of her power and her magic. Her most recent ex (aka, Mr. Sprinkler) was her very first partner since beginning her journey with sacred intimacy. I explained her increased orgasmic potential had more to do with the work she had done on herself and less to do with this man who happened to walk into her life at this critical point.

I assured her that he was only a mirror showing her what was possible for her pleasure, but she owned her orgasmic potential. A week later she called me to share that she had a new lover. "You were right," she exclaimed! She excitedly gushed that their lovemaking was even more amazing and orgasmic than with her ex!

I learned this lesson early in my sex-plorations. The first man I had sex with was nothing special. He wasn't even my boyfriend, although I wanted him to be. He was gloriously uncommitted and I was innocently obsessed with him. It was one-way puppy love. I remember the way he kissed me on my neck felt orgasmic, which is important because I never actually had an orgasm during any of our sexual interactions. But I never wanted to leave him, even though he wouldn't commit to me, solely because I thought *what if no one else can make me feel this good while kissing my neck? I can't risk the potential loss of this pleasure. He must be* the one *because of how good it feels*. Thankfully he was a couple years my senior and went out of state for college, freeing up my heart to explore other connections – truly orgasmic ones. And I started to get a sense that there was so much more out there than the elementary tingles of neck smooches. I graduated from collar kisses to cunnilingus, commitment, and beyond!

It was a series of little steps, one at a time, that led me to a precipice where I began to understand the truly infinite potential of intimacy, connection, and sex. I learned about moving energy with tantric principles of sound, breath, and movement. I discovered and experimented with sex magic. I experienced sacred intimacy as an infinite ocean to explore – I could play on the surface of lots of different lineages and practices OR I could dive deep and lose myself in the wilds of unknown and inexplicable existence. It became my primary spiritual practice and my most beloved science experiment, attempting to find the limits of my potential when channeling my pro-creative energy.

I have shared many stories of wondrous creations, breakthroughs, growth, and healing resulting from my curiosities in exploring life force throughout this book, and there are plenty more juicy ones (see the chapter 12). Some sound downright contradictory, such as overcoming physical ailments by having sex. Seriously, anytime I feel a headache or cold coming on,

I have sex with myself or enroll my partner in Tantra time. As we've learned, everything is energy. And it is dis-ease of the energetic body that manifests as physical disease. I can't say having sex has cured me of every ailment. Yet, I think it's a little more than suspicious that once I felt a UTI (Urinary Tract Infection) coming on and I asked my boyfriend at the time to go down on me and stimulate my g-spot. Post squirting, my symptoms were suddenly gone! I believe the symptoms were a result of energetic contraction, leading to literal contraction of my pelvic floor. Orgasm brought me into a space of surrender and deep relaxation physically and energetically.

Other times, I've been in deep confusion about my personal life, love life, or purpose. Wizards have crystal balls... and I have a crystal dildo! In moments where I have felt beside myself looking for clarity and answers, I have turned to my crystal dildo as a last-ditch effort to find a breakthrough. As if on cue, at the peak of orgasm, I'll usually have a light bulb moment of clarity as pleasure ripples through my body, and if not immediately, within a few days a new book or person or other perspective will seem to fall from the sky and into my life with all the answers I've been looking for. This is how I came up with the name for my podcast, *Talk Tantra to Me*. It's also how I overcame my inner critic in publishing the first episode of the podcast! I was swimming in self-doubt, so I turned to my favorite obsidian crystal dildo. Just as I orgasmed, the awareness *it's not about you* came into my consciousness. *That's right... it's not about me... this work is for the world.* I set my ego aside and launched the thing because God said the world needed it.

Another time, a few years ago, I was working on my abundance mindset. I had just moved into a new home, which also upgraded my living expenses. It was a growth edge for me to be spending so much on rent, but it was absolutely necessary to get a bigger space for my business to grow. I needed space to take clients and host events, but it brought me back into a space of living month to month financially. I was in survival mode and I knew I didn't have to be. So I set a date with myself. I had a glass of wine, ran a bath, and ended with an extended self-pleasure session. Instead of asking the universe for more money, I asked the universe to show me where I had scarcity or lack mindset around money. A couple of days later, I went on a first date. My date was playing big with the menu – ordering bottles of champagne and truffle shavings on what felt like every dish. Throughout the dinner I was doing a mental calculation of the massively growing bill. A part of me was a bit activated. *Am I expected to pay for half of all these luxuries he keeps ordering? Will he pay? It's hard to know on a first date...*

The mental gymnastics I put myself through is evidence enough of my limiting beliefs and scarcity mindset at the time. It was so pervasive that I couldn't be fully present for all the rich decadence on my plate. Then, the bill came. Lo and behold, he grabbed it immediately but didn't open the little book, keeping the receipt and total hidden from both of us. "I'm paying... but I want to play a little game first," he said. He asked me to guess what the total was. He explained that when he's out with his friends, they all guess the total and whoever is closest decides who pays.

I was triggered. Squirming in my seat, thinking, *He wants me to guess the total to show off how much the dinner was. So flashy and tacky.* But this was just my first, unconscious reaction. My higher self was observing these thoughts and called BS – my distrustful perspective was a shadowy projection of unconscious beliefs about wealthy people and men. At the end of the day, this man wanted to provide for me and play a little game while doing it. I was taking it all too seriously, which was showing up in all the other ways I perceived money and abundance. All of this processed within my brain in mere moments. I recognized this was the breakthrough I had asked the universe for a few days before. I shook it off then and there, then we both made our guesses for the total. Of course my guess was more accurate, as I had spent the date tallying his indulgences. He paid, as he said he would regardless of who won, but I won more than his little game that night – I also conquered a bit of my shadow, shedding light on a limiting belief that no longer served me.

This is just one example of the transformative power of sex.

Infinity and beyond became my motto as I explored the delight of many men (and some women) and their unique ways of meeting me. Now I explore infinity and beyond in partnership, as we consistently broaden our range of intimacy and connection. It is truly divine. All of it. In earlier chapters I shared that my first tantric sex experience was totally unintentional (at least on my part). I think a lot of us begin having restorative and transformational sex by accident – or, more specifically, because **that is actually our nature.** When we get out of our heads and into our bodies with true presence, fireworks are inevitable. When we become self-aware and conscious, we organically heal from our trauma and let go of beliefs, patterns, and conditionings that no longer serve us. We become present and we attract partners at a similar vibration. Having intentional sex is more about surrendering to our true nature. It's about unlearning, remembering and coming into our bodies, allowing them to be as magical as God intended.

Think about all the times you've had sex in which you felt like you met God or healed your relationship or changed your perspective on the depths of pleasure you're capable of or just generally felt healthier and happier after. Think about the first time you had sex like that – I hope it was also the first time you had sex and every time after that, but from my experience of the world, I believe that is exceptionally rare, if not totally delusional. The first time you had truly restorative or transformative sex was likely unintentional and a very happy surprise. Probably many times after that, it was also unintentional. Possibly, every time you've had restorative or transformational sex has felt like a joyous coincidence. But imagine the possibilities when you become more intentional, by setting standards for your intimacy and consciously communicating to create what you deeply desire.

Imagine what could happen if you brought in intention; if you decided every sexual experience gets you closer to your highest self and God.

HOMEPLAY
Sacred Sex Ed integration activities and expansive opportunities to transform the way you make love to life.

A PLEASURE PRAYER

Supplies: body oil/lube, self-pleasure toys, and a comfy place to connect to yourself

1. Try calling in a "light bulb moment" in heightened states of arousal. This pleasure practice is similar to a sex magic ritual, in that you are encouraged to connect to the infinite potential of the universe, yet the intention is focused on some place in your life in which you'd like divine guidance, clarity, or a new perspective. This can be done as a solo or partnered ritual.

2. Set an intention. My advice is to consider any places where you feel "stuck" or would like some divine wisdom.

3. Lean into the energy of the universe supporting you. Consider calling forth your highest self, spirit guides, or any divine deity or archetype you identify with.

4. Awaken your Eros. Seduce yourself or each other with full presence and pleasure. Don't rush straight towards genitals. The more you're able to build this energy with edging or waves of arousal, the stronger your life force becomes.

5. Merge intention with Eros at climax. At climax, especially as you orgasm and immediately after, bring the intention, question, or desire for guidance to the front of your mind.

6. Objectively observe any feelings, visualizations, sensations, thoughts, etc. that may come through in the following moments. Let go of attachment – hold space for whatever is available. Expecting guidance to come through in an obvious or familiar way may distract you from other possibilities.

7. Be mindful over the next week as well. Often the universe will deliver clari-ty through an outside source, such as a person, book, challenge, or otherwise.

CHAPTER 8:
CONSCIOUS COMMUNICATION & RADICAL HONESTY

The first time a partner asked me what I like in bed *before* we got into bed, I was sort of triggered. We were having a very hot make-out session in his beat-up car, pulled to the side of the road overlooking the Pacific Ocean and Camps Bay in Cape Town, South Africa. When he pulled back to ask me *what turned me on... what got me off... what I liked*, I felt put on the spot and a bit confused. *He should just know what I like... I don't want to explain it. He must be bad in bed if he has to ask me.*

I legitimately thought men were supposed to read my mind. Guess what this led to? A whole lot of frustrating sexual experiences and resentment. I give myself a lot of grace for the assumption that men should just know, as I wasn't offered a script or any positive examples from my sex education or the media. Hollywood sex scenes and porn alike show couples getting down and dirty with such urgency, and often unrealistic exclamations from the female performers, who have had little to no foreplay or stimulation. I also wasn't even aware how much my body and desires change from day to day, as is typical for women, due to our cyclical natures. Now I am able to track that the slow sex I want right before my period starts is very different from the primal desires I have at peak ovulation. Thanks to our rotating hormonal shifts, women can bring a wide range of sexual appetite.

It feels very cringey for me to admit, but I used to fake orgasms. I used to tolerate penetration that was too hard and fast before I was wet and open. I used to have my boundaries violated A LOT because I was too afraid to say "no." I had a lot of bad sex – and it was mostly my fault. I was giving away all my power by staying quiet and small. I was the victim of my sexuality, rather than a conscious creator.

I look back on the memory of my lover's adorably innocent desire to please me as a catalyst of a new empowering chapter in my sexuality. As far as I remember, I don't think I even authentically answered his question. I believe I froze, things were awkward for a minute, and then I attempted some dirty talk, misinterpreting his genuine care as a desire for whore-ific word play. But a seed was planted and now I'm sovereign in my sex. I know what I like and I ask for it outright. I don't worry about hurting my lover's feelings, because I know I'm actually doing them a favor. I'm gifting them the cheat code to my body. If I'm feeling discomfort or pain, I ask to change positions or slow down or pause. *I trust we'll both be better off when I feel juicy instead of contracted.* I communicate my boundaries before we make it to the bedroom. I feel safe and present, knowing that my needs and fears have been heard.

When it comes to communication, we need to recognize its weight as a primary tool for co-creation. All relationships are co-creations, whether it is with a friend, lover, family member, life partner, or otherwise. Ideally we are consciously using these relationships to create growth together, but relationships can also be used to create comfort zones where we can live in the illusion of our limiting patterns and beliefs, or to create harm. Either way you're creating something, you can do that consciously or unconsciously. You can create cohesion, peace, empowerment, and love, or you can create fear, separation, and pain.

All acts of creation are expressions of our current emotional state. When we consider the act of creating, we often associate it with artistic endeavors such as painting, dancing, or writing... but **creation is happening in every moment of our lives.** Every decision we make is a creative decision, usually based on how we're currently feeling or how we would like to feel. We decide what foods to eat, what clothes we wear, and how we have we sex; in the process, we are creating ourselves in that moment and expressing our state of being. The people we choose to spend time with have a big impact on our creative potential. They're co-creators in our reality, as their decisions impact our own.

If we're not communicating our highest truth, we're missing the mark in regard to the greatest potential of our relationships. We are often recycling our emotions or projecting them unconsciously, rather than using them as data to consciously create together. E-motion is energy in motion, and energy is information. Our emotions are giving us the low-down of what is working for us and what is not. When we meet our emotions with curiosity – like a scientist looking at the data – we are empowered to decide our next moves with conscious creation in the lead and we communicate this to the world with authenticity. We become conscious creators of our reality.

Unfortunately for most of us, this isn't our default way of being. We have a deep fear of our emotions because they've been made out to be "bad." Most of us aren't taught how to process and communicate our emotions in healthy ways. We're told to *be quiet... grow up... stop crying... don't be a baby.* Even exuberant and positive emotions may be met with *settle down... snorting is impolite... you're being too loud... go to your room with that.* Additionally, many public education systems are actively cutting art, music, and physical education programs, which are some of the only places where children are encouraged to express and release pent-up emotions.

Our elders and caregivers were doing the best with what they had, but very few of us have been given the opportunities and space to see the power and gift of our emotions. For years I stifled my emotional expression and plastered a smile on my face. It wasn't until I discovered Tantra that I found the tools to excavate the bottled-up emotions. What came next was a tsunami of feelings. Years and years of pent-up rage and sadness crashed to the surface. I felt it. I held it. I let it flow and let it go. But there was also a part of me holding judgment for the expression of the fullness of my humanity.

The more you get in touch with your true feelings, the greater your ability to get in touch with your highest truth and communicate it. **Your highest truth is synonymous with your highest love.** Your highest truth is an expression of beingness that has the potential to bring the greatest love and positive evolution to the world. Your highest love and highest truth are not martyrs or people pleasers – they are in it for the highest good of all, *especially you.*

TRUSTING YOUR TRUTH

We often withhold our highest truth, tell white lies, or skirt around uncomfy topics in the name of "love." We don't want to share our truth with the people we love and care about, because we fear our truth will hurt them or it will make them not love us, and then leave us. We're afraid to hurt their feelings or be alone, so we cushion it or avoid the conversation all together, but withholding your truth is actually the opposite of love. Truly unconditional love sets us free. When we are operating from divine love, we are willing to have the hard conversations. When we share our truth, it may absolutely "hurt their feelings" in the moment, but what you're actually bruising is their ego or their human, *not their soul.*

This can be a difficult pill to swallow, given the likely reality that our truth *will* trigger the people we love, which means the potential crunchiness of watching our loved ones process and work through the fun-comfortable (uncomfortable, but also fun because we're growing and doing the hard things for a greater reward!) emotions. On the other side, this truth can only set one free because *triggers are actually initiations into our highest selves.* They are an invitation to heal and an opportunity to gain new perspective or clarity. Triggers offer the opportunity to love and accept ourselves and our realities more fully. This is not an easy feat and comes down to self-awareness and shadow work. When we trigger someone with our truth, we are inviting them to take a closer look at their own truth. It is in the trigger where our hidden truths lie, calling out for our attention in the form of an upset.

Let me give you a very clear example. Let's say you have a child who is a drug addict. Their life is in shambles and they're on the fast track to create real damage in their lives. As a parent, it is heartbreaking to witness. You deeply desire to see them happy and thriving. They come to you asking for money.

Would it be truly unconditional love to give them $100? If you really think about it, *how do you honestly believe that money would be spent?*

To most people reading, it's pretty obvious that in this circumstance blindly giving the child money would likely not be in anyone's highest good. That money would likely perpetuate the cycle of abuse. *What would be unconditionally loving?* Perhaps having an intervention or setting boundaries would support them most. Sitting down with the child to share how their drug addiction has impacted their family might provide the empathy they need to break through. Offering to take them to rehab or letting them know it is unacceptable for them to come around the house while they are using can be a powerful expression of love. While it may be difficult and even heartbreaking to say this to your child, this dialogue is the most loving course of action. While it may be triggering or frustrating for your child to have this kind of intervention, it is also gifting them a moment of truth and love. You are mirroring a grander version of their life. You are setting them free to the truth of their potential and what you see in them. You are calling them forth.

Other circumstances may be more complex. For example, sharing your desires or boundaries in and out of the bedroom can bring up a lot of fear... *What if they think I'm weird? What if they reject me? What if I don't get what I desire? What if I do?* One of the most vulnerable things we can do is tell someone we love them. Many of us struggle to even tell our parents and family we love them, let alone a new romantic partner. Putting our hearts on the line is the ultimate vulnerability. **Vulnerability is to be naked in your highest truth and grandest soul expression.** It is a holy contradiction of risk and reward. When we are truly vulnerable, we drop the ego in favor of trusting ourselves and spirit with strength in surrender. Being vulnerable involves sharing your highest truth and trusting the most aligned possible outcome with the greatest degree of expansion and freedom to unfold.

Sometimes this means letting go of the relationship entirely or allowing it to self-combust on its own. I once fell deeply in love with a man who had originally applied to work with me. We had an intake call to talk about my offerings, but instead sparks were flying. By the end of it, we were both clear that we wanted to date rather than pursue the professional relationship he had originally intended. I felt so validated in the relationship. I was barely a year into my career as a tantrika and only a couple months "out" and publicly sharing my work. At that time, I felt it was a big risk to follow this career path, because I worried it would automatically scare off a lot of perfectly eligible dudes. So when this one came in love-bombing all over me, I was so relieved. We had met because of the work I was doing in the world with hands-on sexual bodywork, and *he* had decided to pursue *me* knowing this! I was looking externally for my partners to validate my worthiness for love. I wanted them to say, "I still love you, even though you've been raped. I love you even more because of the work you do – you are so powerful!"

But as soon as I became comfortable with his validation, I felt it begin to slip away. I felt a distance between us emerging. I wasn't quite sure he could hold all of me. I sensed he wasn't ready for the deep commitment of a growth-oriented relationship. We came to that inevitable fulcrum point in the relationship, where we would either go deep or he would have to get out of my waters.

One night he picked me up and we went on a nighttime drive into the Hollywood Hills to appreciate the city lights below. I made us cacao, which we sipped from a thermos. I vulnerably shared more about my work, my history with sexual assault, and my feelings about him. I asked him what he thought of our relationship. It was a stretch for me to lay it all out – the vulnerability of radical honesty made my stomach do flips, but I also felt so relieved to be so honest about my feelings and intentions. To let go and let the universe unfold the highest path for me. I didn't know what the outcome would be of sharing it all, but I certainly trusted my highest truth to bring the highest love.

To be honest, I don't remember much of what he said in response, likely because it was mostly short, placating responses. The next day I left for Hawaii for a week and he ghosted me. There's no better place to be stewing in an emotional hangover than the island of Maui. Her gorgeous landscapes and incredible biodiversity held me in my heartache, as I began to disentangle the meaning I had given this relationship. His sudden lack of communication made me feel unlovable. I had bared my heart and he rejected it. I created the story in my mind that my sexual assault scared him away and I would never get the love I desired because I was damaged. I felt tinges of regret, but I chose to lean into new expressions of self-love. It was an important moment for me in choosing to validate myself. Then and there, I began to embody and believe the truth that I am inherently loveable and my humanness and history only added to my worthiness.

Ghosting can feel especially traumatic and may lead to us to become even more fearful of sharing our truth in forthcoming situations. The inner critic within me desired to use the ghosting as "proof" that I was indeed unlovable and unworthy, but thankfully my higher self stayed to soothe my grief and transform my breakdown into breakthrough.

When someone rejects our truth, has an outsized reaction, or ghosts us, we often think, *What did I do? What could I have done differently that would have this person still communicating with me? What could I have changed that would make them still want to talk to me?* We have to stop this spiraling in its tracks, because it's really not about us. It's more likely that they just don't know how to communicate. They may not even be connected to their highest truth or aware of what they really want. And almost certainly, they don't always feel safe expressing their emotions, just like me (and maybe you?!). And unlike me and you, they are unwilling to take the risk of vulnerability to *go there* or aren't even aware it is a viable option. So when it comes to sharing our highest truth, it is important to recognize that not everyone will be able to meet you there – but you are planting a seed. You are giving them evidence of what is possible in terms of communication and emotional expression. What a gift!

And what a gift that their inability to meet you there *sets you free*. It sets you free to the reality of where they're at; it sets you free to decide how invested you'd like to be in the connection, to set new boundaries or redirect your energy to connections that can actually receive all of you – connections that feel more expansive and growth-oriented. This man ghosting me was the best gift he could give me, because it set me free to find a man who could hold all of my truth, even the messiest parts of me.

Finally, it's important to recognize that your truth may not always feel "true" for the other, and their truth may not feel "true" for you. That doesn't mean one person is right and the other is wrong. We are all bringing unique world experiences, perspectives, preferences, and priorities to the table. Be conscious of any tendency to throw your emotions at the other and label it as your "truth." We can fall into the trap of believing the other cannot hold all of us or are unloving, when in reality there is an opportunity for us to take greater responsibility for our emotions and acknowledge that more than one perspective can exist. This is especially important to be mindful of if you find yourself in a pattern of relationships where you don't feel met. There can be a tendency to remove someone from our lives when there is conflict, rather than using the conflict as an opportunity to learn and grow together. When we set our ego aside, we are much more likely to come to the realization that we don't actually want to be right – we want to love and to be loved. We want to respect the other and be respected.

HOW TO HAVE A CLEARING CONVERSATION

1. Get grounded
Set an intention. From a place of love, feel into a desired outcome of clearing the space to build, repair, or evolve the relationship. Enter open-minded, ready to release resentment or guilt.

2. Consent
Start by asking the "other" if/when they have space for a deep conversation.

3. Share intention
Why are we bringing this up? For clarity? Compassion? To set a boundary? To become closer? To build trust? To evolve the relationship? Own your fears and insecurities.
Example: *My intention is to share vulnerably about how I've been feeling about xyz – to feel heard and seen. I hope this invites you to share your feelings so we can understand each other better.*

4. Share your heart
What happened (witout shame or blame – own your feelings)?
Example: *What I'm avoiding speaking to you about is* I was triggered by you not texting me back. *I experienced a feeling of* sadness and anger.

5. Tell your stories
Take responsibility for your part AND your stories. What did you make their actions or words mean about you, them, or the relationship? Own your fears and insecurities. Your vulnerability is likely to open their heart and inspire them to share their own deeper truth.
Example: *The story I made up about myself is that* I'm unworthy of love. *The story I made up about you is that* you don't care about me.

6. Renegotiate the relationship
Ask for what you need and offer ways you can respond more productively in the future.
Example: *I take responsibility for* assuming you knew what I needed. *I apologize for* punishing you by making snarky comments. *I would like*

to request we talk about how often we check in with one another. *Do you have any requests for me?*

7. Pro Tip: Use the exact dialogue above, just sub out the un-italicized portion with your own pieces. You could even share this with those you relate with frequently to simplify your conflict resolution.

8. Bonus Tip: Before having a clearing convo, make sure you are well-nourished, meaning you are fed, well-slept, and generally feeling good physically and energetically (aside from potential discomfort caused by the conflict at hand). Taking care of yourself empowers you to be present and well-resourced instead of re-active in hard conversations and before big decisions. If we haven't taken care of our basic needs, we are starting off in survival mode, which could lead to an even more explosive conflict and less resolution. Set yourself up for success by prioritizing nourishment.

VULNERABILITY AND "MESS" INSPIRES DEPTH

When I met my husband, Andrew, he had recently made a pretty big mess in his interpersonal relationships, of which I was privy to because of our overlapping circle of friends. It's not my story to tell, but in essence, I identified the mess he created as a result of him not feeling safe or nourished to share his truth or own his deeper desires. So he reverted to unhealed behaviors – he was doing his best based on where he was at the time, but he's also human. I saw it all playing out with a high level of compassion and grace, knowing I'd been there too. From the get-go, Andrew was very honest and upfront with me about the mistakes he made and what he was doing to clean it up. It actually made me fall in love with him faster. *If this is how he shows up when he fucks up, I'm on board,* I thought. His integrity, authenticity, and radical honesty inspired me to be vulnerable with him. I was able to receive him at his worst and still love him, and I hoped he'd be able to do the same for me. So over dinner on our third date, I shared the worst thing I ever did.

I told him about the time I cheated on my ex, Joseph*. I shared how I didn't feel safe to explore what I really wanted in that relationship, let alone ask for it. I was very hurt and terrified Joseph would leave me. So I succumbed to shadowy desires... I subconsciously put myself in a situation with a different man who felt more open, spiritual, and evolved so I could play with the alternatives. The cheating was mostly emotional, meaning we never had sex, but I toed the line very closely with cuddles, kisses on the neck, and some heavy petting. It was not my finest moment and I learned a lot from it. It was the equivalent of Andrew's interpersonal drama. So I told him the whole story, unprompted, on our third date. I was terrified he would run the other direction, get angry, or hold it over my head. Instead, he told me how much he loved me and how much he appreciated me for being so forthcoming. He said it made him trust me more to share something so vulnerable and potentially destructive so early in the relationship.

Then and there I knew I could tell Andrew anything. And he felt the same way. Our relationship was built on the foundations of radical honesty and responsibility, even when it's really, really hard. We don't do it all perfectly, but one thing I'm very proud of in our relationship is that nothing is left unsaid.

But how do we discover what our highest truth actually is?

Very often we feel confused or unsure of our truth. I believe this is the case because we have been conditioned to look outside of ourselves for the truth *and/or* we may have been taught that our authentic self is bad or wrong because it doesn't fit into societal expectations. Equally possible, we don't believe what we desire is even possible for us. For example, with my ex, Joseph (the one I cheated on), I was comparing our relationship to those I saw on TV and in my life, when in reality I wanted to create a relationship that was very non-traditional. I wanted more freedom to explore other connections but was terrified to ask for it because, deep down, I didn't believe it was possible for us. I was terrified to even own the desire for myself, because I was living in scarcity... *If I let go of this man whom I love and loves me, what if I never find another?* So I totally bypassed my truth and lied to myself about the viability and potential longevity of our relationship.

Connecting and living in alignment with our highest truth requires a high degree of trust and surrender. Sharing your highest truth brings you closer to those who are meant to be in your life and closer to the most authentic versions of ourselves. Sharing your highest truth, especially if it is vulnerable or triggering, is like bearing your soul and asking, "Can you love all of me?"

HOMEPLAY
Sacred Sex Ed integration activities and expansive opportunities to transform the way you make love to life.

HIGHEST LOVE JOURNAL EXERCISE
Supplies: pen and paper

1. Consider three desires, lifestyle choices, or topics you fear addressing with a partner, family member, or friends.

2. Then consider how you could communicate this to them compassionately.

3. Finally, zoom out and consider how sharing this info will set you AND the other free. Consider asking yourself, *How could sharing my truth bring more vulnerability or connection? How could it give them permission to find their truth?*

4. (Example: I'm afraid to tell my partner I want to quit my job and start my dream business. I fear they will not support this desire because of the potential strain on the relationship or on our finances. But maybe sharing this truth will create space for new perspectives and problem solving. Maybe they will see potential for greater joy in our lives. Maybe it will give them permission to consider if they're fulfilled in their job...)

- 3 things I'm afraid to express...

- How could expressing this truth set myself and the other free?

CHAPTER 9:

SEXY CONSENT SKILLS

Consent is SO sexy. But I didn't always think so. Communicating in the bedroom used to really challenge and confuse me. I believed it ruined the mood. Maybe you relate? We're conditioned to believe sex and intimacy should be entirely spontaneous. And honestly, the thought of pausing mid-hook-up to awkwardly mumble, "Can I stick it in?" still makes my stomach turn.

But consent CAN be sexy. Mostly because *communicating our desires and boundaries allows us to get out of our heads and into our bodies.* Think about it. When we take the time to say, "I like this..." we're not in our heads thinking, *I wish she would...* When we take the time to say, "I'm not feeling up to penetration..." we're not worried about him inching his hand closer and closer to our pussy. When we take the lead and ask our partners what they desire and what's feeling off limits, we drastically minimize the risk of getting caught in a "me too" moment and we create space for healing in our partnerships.

In 2017, the #MeToo movement went viral as individuals all over the world vulnerably shared their stories of sexual exploitation, harassment, and assault. Having been a survivor of all the above, I hold so much tenderness for the women and men who have come forward to illustrate the pervasive nature of sexual violence in modern culture.

Men and women have different biological urges and evolutionary responsibility in their genetic makeup – this is just how it is. Studies back up the data that men are statistically more likely to be perpetrators of sexual violence and women are more likely to be victims. It is my belief that sexual violence is so pervasive not because men are inherently bad, but because most men have not been taught how to ask for consent AND because most women have not been taught how to say no, or how to ask for, or even know what we want *for that matter.* It is the latter that I believe is not addressed or talked about enough.

While the inverse is true as well – meaning women have also not been taught how to ask for consent and men are not educated on how to express their boundaries – I find the way girls and boys are socialized and conditioned to be drastically different and necessary to address. Whether it is biological or socially conditioned, by and large men tend to be the curators of a sexual experience, meaning they are encouraged and motivated to make the first move, implying they should also be the leaders in asking for consent. And women tend to be more receptive, meaning they get to communicate what they desire and what is off limits. More and more women and men are becoming comfortable and confident in reversing these roles, which further demonstrates the concept that we all have both masculine and feminine energy within us.

However most of us were conditioned in a world where women are usually the more emotionally sensitive sex. This is supported by evolutionary biology, in that women *needed* to evolve to be nurturers to continue our species. Women are often further conditioned to be people-pleasing and placating to avoid hurting feelings, maintain the interest and attraction of the male, and keep peace within the family unit. For this reason, speaking her mind, especially when it goes against the grain, can feel very uncomfortable. This shows up in the inverse as well and across non-binary, LGBTQ+ relationships. In these cases, one individual (regardless of gender and sexual orientation) usually takes on a more energetically penetrating masculine role and the other takes the receptive feminine role.

From the #MeToo movement, we find there is ample opportunity to empower survivors and educate the next generations on how to avoid being a perpetrator. And it simply comes down to communicating and respecting one another. The majority of sexual trauma comes from the perception of our boundaries being crossed or judgment of our desires. Sometimes we don't even have a chance to communicate our boundaries before they are crossed, making it even more confusing! Other times, we fear setting boundaries in our relationships (whether with our partner, family, friends, or in work) out of fear that we will be abandoned or replaced by someone without boundaries. Boundaries contribute to a safe container for co-creation in all types of relationships.

Beyond protecting ourselves from being involved in any capacity of sexual violence, consent skills are also the key to expanded orgasmic potential. Deep down, we need to feel safe. *We can't truly receive pleasure until we are in a regulated space.* We can't be incredibly spontaneous until we know we're not going to accidentally create some irreversible consequence. *What do we need to feel safe?* We need to communicate with one another. We need to ask for consent and take responsibility for our bodies and our pleasure.

From my personal experience and having witnessed and guided thousands of individuals in erotic settings, the number one thing that hinders pleasure and keeps orgasms at bay is being stuck in our heads. It's far too easy to get caught in mind drama instead of being present for the pleasure available in moments of intimacy. When we communicate our desires and boundaries before intimate encounters, we feel safe to let go of the mind drama and enjoy the pleasure coursing through our bodies.

HERE ARE TIPS TO DO SO WITHOUT TAKING THE SEXY OUT OF SAFER-SEX CONVERSATIONS:

1. **Make it a part of the foreplay.** Instead of perceiving consent as a box that needs to be checked, introduce desires over dinner. This is like preheating the oven for super hot intimacy. Consider phrases like, *"What turns you on?"* or turn up the heat with something like, *"What do you want to do to me?"* Use these phrases to direct the conversation into boundaries. For example, I may respond to one of these questions with, *"I'm really into kink and BDSM, but I save it for partners whom I have an established relationship with... so let's table that for tonight. But I'd love some sensual connection. What about you?"*

2. Pleasure creates an altered state of consciousness because it triggers the release of "happy hormones" such as serotonin, dopamine, endorphins, and oxytocin. Plant medicines, drugs, and alcohol also alter our consciousness, partly by secreting similar hormones. It is relevant to

consider, you may make different decisions when *under the influence of arousal,* just like you might under the influence of substances.

3. For this reason, I recommend considering your *non-negotiables* before even going into a date. Non-negotiables are hard boundaries or needs that must be established for connection to happen. Your non-negotiables could be no sex without a condom... or it could be no kisses on the first date... or you need to orgasm at least once before penetration. Consider the pacing, desires, and boundaries which feel important to you. If intimacy becomes available on the date, honor yourself and the non-negotiables you identified with yourself.

It is perfectly acceptable and encouraged to evoke additional boundaries or non-negotiables during the date, but I do not recommend revoking them. **Revoking boundaries or non-negotiables while you are in the altered state of pleasure may lead to regret down the line and distrust of your own ability to create safety for yourself.** We are not living in scarcity; there will be further opportunities for you to connect sensually or sexually. You are invited to renegotiate boundaries/non-negotiables before the next encounter, while you are in a present and un-altered state. Those who are unwilling to honor you and your boundaries are not worthy of meeting the divine that is your yoni-pussy or lingam-cock.

4. Consider every "rejection" a "redirection." Don't take boundaries or desires personally. If something you desire is not available for this coupling, get curious about what else is available OR what you can do to create space and safety to get closer to making that desire a reality down the line. There are infinite reasons someone may be a "no" to connecting in the way you desire and at least half of them have nothing to do with you. Also, if someone is a "yes" on one occasion, do not assume they are always a "yes." Give each other the grace and sovereignty to feel into your sacred "yes" and "no" in each moment. If your partner makes a request for something other than what you're currently serving, don't assume you're doing it wrong or you're not a good lover. Applaud them for giving you the cheat code to their body. For example, if they ask you to slow down or go harder, don't read into it. It is incredibly courageous to share our desires. What a gift when our lovers educate us on how to love them best in that moment.

5. Women have especially beautiful complexities. Female hormonal patterns follow the lunar cycle, meaning, just like the moon, she has phases. What turns her on will likely differ day to day. For example, I tend to be much more interested in trying new, kinky things around my ovulation, and desire sweet, slow, tantric sex before my period. How cool is it that she is a different woman in bed each day? And you get to treat her body like the grandest and most rewarding exploration.

Men, on the other hand, follow a solar cycle, meaning his turn on is more predictable at certain times of the day, everyday (for most men, they feel aroused in the morning, i.e. morning wood, when testosterone levels are highest). For those with fluidity in their sex and/or gender, hormonal influence on desire may fall anywhere between these two extremes that traditionally characterize biological men and women. If you or a lover falls on the fluid spectrum, get curious and consider having a conversation about it. Regardless, external factors, such as celebration and stress, can greatly influence the sensual appetite in all sexes and genders.

6. Be playful. Most of the weight, seriousness, and awkwardness we put on eroticism is conditioned by our elders, church, and society. Let that shit go. Give yourself permission to try something new, to be silly, and to laugh along the way. Consider approaching your intimate moments as if you are a teenager exploring naked bodies for the first time, or even consider yourself a child at the playground. There is SO much more available in sex than just penis in vagina. Sex is sacred play.

I've found taking penetration off the table can be a powerful practice in opening the partnership up to incredibly juicy energetic and sensual play that we would have otherwise bypassed had we rushed to the finish line. When clients share that everything is "great" in their relationship except the lack of passion or chemistry, I congratulate them. In my experience, sexual intimacy is one of the easiest things to fix in relationships; however, it can sometimes be a symptom of other underlying and unaddressed issues. Yet, if a couple truly is compatible in every other way, especially with communication, I ask them to take that to the bedroom. Slow way down, get curious, and make laughter the goal, instead of orgasm.

HOW TO HAVE SAFER SEX CONVERSATIONS

Once upon a time, I made a New Year's resolution to communicate my needs, preferences, and boundaries before each new intimate counter. Nowadays, this is a no brainer, but when I feel into the version of myself that made this declaration, it feels super stretchy. I didn't know if I could really trust myself to have what I perceived as a very uncomfortable conversation. But I did it anyway. It was uncomfortable at first, but it became easier and easier. I honestly can't remember a single potential lover that was resistant to the conversation. Most were grateful, surprised, or curious. More than one expressed something along the lines of, "I never thought of having a conversation like this… but I love it." I smile with pride at the seeds planted with those lovers, hoping they've spread the gospel like wildfire to their forthcoming connections.

The more sexually literate I became through my healing journey, the clearer I became on my desires and boundaries. I became more conscious of what I needed to know about my lovers before I felt safe to let them near my temple. One common framework which supports safer-sex conversations is SPREAD. SPREAD is an acronym that perfectly encapsulates all the considerations for a safer-sex interaction:

S – Sexual health STI panels, and risky behaviors
P – Protection/pregnancy and preferences/pronouns
R – Relationship status, style, and agreements
E – Emotions, "What does this mean for you?"
A – Aftercare needs and expectations
D – Decide, communicate desires/fears/boundaries

You don't need to have a SPREAD conversation in the exact order listed above, but the acronym is meant to help us recall important factors in consideration for sexual connections.

S stands for sexual health, and it covers questions like: *When were you last tested for STIs? What for? What were the results? Have you had unprotected sex since then?*

P stands for protection, pregnancy, and pronouns. It covers questions like: *How do you feel about condoms? Are you on birth control? How would we move forward if this interaction resulted in pregnancy? What are your pronouns?* If you/they are trans or non-binary, *How would you prefer for me to refer to your genitals?*

R stands for relationship status, agreements with partners, and relating style. It covers questions like: *Will anyone in your life be affected by our connection? Are you polyamorous, monogamous, or somewhere in between? Does your partner know and consent to you having other connections? Are there any boundaries you've agreed to with your partner which would affect how we connect? Are you open to exploring a relationship beyond this connection?*

E stands for emotions, and it covers questions like: *What does this mean for you? Do you need an emotional connection to explore sexual intimacy? What are your intentions for this connection and beyond?*

A stands for aftercare needs and expectations. It covers questions like: *How can I support you after we share intimacy? Would you like me to text or call you tomorrow to check in? Would you like to cuddle after or do you need space?*

D stands for decision. Finally, once you have all the info, you are empowered to make a truly informed decision as to how you'd like to connect with someone. Based on all the information, you can *express your desires* (what type of connection is on the table), *address your fears* (share any lingering considerations), and *communicate boundaries* (create safety and trust by communicating what is off limits).

While it is useful to have all considerations listed clearly, your SPREAD convos don't need to come off like a laundry list. Invite in playfulness and sensuality. When we share things like our sexual health status, emotional needs, desire for protection, etc., we feel *clear*, meaning we aren't in our heads so much and are able to be truly present for forthcoming intimacy. It's all on the table and there's no confusion. I used to feel so awkward bringing up these factors, but now I find it to be a relief. When I have sex with someone new, I'm not worried about getting an STI or whether or not it's a one-night stand, because everything has been addressed in the SPREAD conversation. We demo how to have safer-sex convos such as this one in a playful and sexy way at our Tantra Retreats and play parties.

As a people pleaser, boundaries have been especially complex for me to fully claim. I hated saying no. I always had.

It seems simple, right? If you don't want to do something, you say, "No thanks – not interested." But it has never been that simple for me. I hated saying no because I equated it with disappointing people. I worried they'd look at me differently. They'd mislabel me. They'd think I was different. Difficult. Prudish. Lazy. I will never be able to count the number of times I've said yes, when I really wanted to say no. And there's been even more times where I just said nothing at all. This goes far beyond my erotic expression.

How we do one thing is how we do everything. I've completed tasks at work I didn't feel comfortable with because I didn't want my bosses or clients to question my loyalty or work ethic. I've gone out with and kissed men I didn't want to because I didn't want them to feel bad or rejected if I said, "*No.*" I drank one too many one too many times because I didn't want to seem prude or uncool. I've risked my life because I wanted to appear fearless. Ironically, all of these decisions were spawned from fear.

Over time, I let go of my fear of judgment, rejection, and reaction. I realized that prioritizing myself was in the best interest of everyone else. I began respecting myself and my self-worth. I became authentically myself. There will always be those who are critical or may push my boundaries, but now I realize those who are threatened by them likely were unjustly benefitting from my disempowerment. I'm confident that the people who really matter will support my decisions. I'm committed to being true to myself and my desires.

And the beautiful thing is that the more empowered I became in my sexual boundaries, the easier it became to set boundaries with my friends, family, work, and every other arena of life. *As above, so below.* Many of us are taught that unconditional love has no boundaries. In reality, setting boundaries can be a great act of love. It is to say, *I am worthy of love so I create space for my safety and soul expression, and You are worthy of knowing my boundaries, so you can love me in the way that will give you the most joy because I will feel safe to receive it.*

On this topic, it is also relevant to address body language and non-verbal communication. Once upon a time, my date shared a desire to give me a massage. I happily obliged. I wasn't ready for sexy time, but a massage felt like a great way to suss out his potential while dropping into my body. I lay naked on the bed and he went for it. Working his way up from my feet, he got closer and closer to my ass and pussy. He was inching nearer as he worked my inner thigh. First I froze… then I began to lean away, signaling I wasn't comfortable. He kept going, suddenly moving fast and getting even closer to my pussy, breathing heavily on my back all the while. I tried creating more space and made noises that signaled my "no." He didn't get the memo. Eventually, I excused myself and stepped into the bathroom for a few deep breaths.

When I returned, I took responsibility for not using my words and shared my perspective of the incident. My date was astonished. He thought I was writhing and moaning in pleasure – not trying to get away and signaling discomfort! It was a big lesson for both of us. For me, to just speak up. And for him, to ask! I do find that once things begin getting hot and heavy, having someone incessantly ask, *How does that feel? Do you like that? What about that? Is this okay?* Can actually take you out of the experience. When in doubt, I recommend asking simple questions that can be answered with one word, such as: *Harder or softer? Slower or faster? Can I touch your cock? Are you ready to have me inside?* Questions that require just one word to answer require less mental capacity so we are more likely to stay embodied in pleasure.

I'm also not advising against non-verbal communication. In fact, as the sexually-educated being you are in reading this book, I believe **there is an even greater duty on your end** of intimate encounters to be aware of micro-shifts in your partner's demeanor. This is done with pure presence and advanced emotional intelligence. Reading our partner's non-verbal cues is generally easier the more time we've spent with them, but those in long-term partnerships are not immune to these sexy consent tools.

In fact, having conversations around desires, fears, and boundaries can be downright liberating for individuals in committed relationships.

Communicating these factors in the safety of a relationship may bring up long-forgotten fantasies, heal past traumas, and reinvigorate chemistry. Our desires and boundaries also shift from day to day. It is incredibly valuable to feel into where you are individually before an intimate encounter.

Regardless of your relationship status, your ability to voice your desires and express your boundaries is likely to transcend the bedroom in a downright delicious way. If you can speak your desires when you are the most physically and emotionally vulnerable, you can do it anywhere.

If you can request him to slow down and devour you gently, you can ask for a raise. If you can ask her to eat your ass, you can ask for freshly sliced tomatoes for your sandwich, instead of those slimy day-old ones. If you can check in with your pussy or cock before you masturbate, you can trust yourself to set boundaries with everyone in your life, from your mom to the stranger in the grocery line to your significant other. If you can communicate your NEED for them to text you tomorrow to check in, you can be ballsy enough to dream your BIG dream... *you know the one I'm talking about.*

But asking for what you want can feel really crunchy if you've never been taught how to do it before or you were taught to take care of everyone else before yourself. Hopefully the tools in this chapter empower you to feel confident and curious about evoking sexy consent skills into your sexual interactions. But just like with everything, practice makes perfect! So go forth and claim your desires! Without expectation and with consent, of course.

HOMEPLAY
Sacred Sex Ed integration activities and expansive opportunities to transform the way you make love to life.

SAFETY IS SEXY
Supplies: optional pen and paper

Creating safety in coupled intimacy is a form of self-care. Non-negotiables are one way to implement greater safety, especially in sexual intimacy. A non-negotiable is something that is an absolute *must* – it is a form of boundary or ultimatum.

Non-sexual examples may include dietary restrictions or the decision not to drink and drive. Sexual examples of non-negotiables may include not being sexually intimate with a new partner if you haven't had a SPREAD conversation or not having sex when you're under the influence of alcohol. Regardless of your non-negotiables, they don't need to be justified, and they are tailored to what feels accessible and empowering for you.

1. Whether you are single and playing the field, in a committed, monogamous relationship, or anywhere in between, consider non-negotiables, especially in regard to communication, that you'd like to implement before partnered intimacy. If you're dating around, you may want to know more, perhaps having an entire SPREAD conversation before getting under the sheets. If you have familiarity with your partner, maybe you want to focus on desires, fears, and boundaries before each sex-ploration.

2. Make this decision in a regulated and unaroused state and commit to it!

3. Actually follow through on this commitment to yourself. Begin having these conversations with your partner or potential partners.

CHAPTER 10:
EXPLORING RELATING STYLES

"You know they're swingers?," my stepmom said in a not-so-hushed voice to my dad as we pulled away from a backyard BBQ. I was 10 years old and it was my first revelation in open-relating. I didn't know what *swingers* were, but it sounded very fun, indeed, despite the clearly judgmental and condescending tone carried around the subject. I badgered my parents to tell me what it meant. I was surprised to learn *swinging* meant this couple (my parents' friends) had sex with people other than each other. It floored me and filled me with curiosity. At that moment, as a sprightly 10-year-old, I had no judgment of the couple or the idea of open-relating. In fact, it made sense to me and sounded fun, even at that age and with my conditioning.

It wasn't until I was in my college years that I began to try open-relating more seriously. I was in a four-year relationship from age 17 to 21. We met at Outback Steakhouse, where we both worked. He was four years older than me and had very little life direction when we first met. But he was my first real love and also the first man to create enough safety for me to experience orgasm with another person – previously I had only had orgasms through self-pleasure. We were together for a year before I moved away to Chicago for school. We managed the long-distance thing, but I was also a young, beautiful college student meeting many very eligible young bachelors. I discovered that talking about my boyfriend back home led to these men ignoring me. Meanwhile, I saw my single friends get lots of free drinks at the bar. So, after a time, I began pretending I was single when I went out. It was a slippery slope and I toed a fine line of faithfulness. More than once a man leaned in for a kiss, and I blurted out, "*I have a boyfriend"* before they had a chance to make their landing.

The summer between my freshman and sophomore year of college, my boyfriend got really drunk and drove his car into a lake. I decided we would *take a break*. On that break, I called up one of the young bachelors I had met on the Gold Coast in Chicago months prior. My friends and I called him Fishy Phil because of the incredibly ornate fish tank he had in his apartment. I remember that on the night I first met him during my freshman year, he lured me and my friends back to his place with the promise that we could feed his precious clownfish. Melanie* and I dropped colorful nutrient flakes into the tank excitedly and then cuddled up with each other on his couch, while he nursed blue balls in the adjacent room. Little did I know, by summer I would find myself sucking his cock under the blue glow of the tank. I slipped into his hockey jersey the next morning as he made me breakfast. It was a fun fling, but my heart ached for the man who was my first real love. A few days later, I scurried back into my boyfriend's arms, confessing the whole thing and asking for repair.

We got back together and he ended up moving to Chicago to be with me in the middle of my sophomore year, but I still longed for the freedom of my single friends, especially after I had a taste of someone new. I read *Sex at Dawn* by Christopher Ryan and Cacilda Jethá, *Ethical Slut* by Janet W. Hardy and Dossie Easton, and several other titles promoting open-relating. I presented my findings to my boyfriend, who immediately shut them down. Meanwhile, in the bedroom at the heights of pleasure, he would conveniently bring up and get off on the idea of me with Fishy Phil. It supported the mounting evidence I had of the natural way of polyamory. The more my partner shut down the potential of us exploring outside the relationship, the more I rebelled and sought attention outside our partnership. We broke up and set each other free to find what we really desired, but I was convinced no heterosexual man would be able to make peace with the idea of his beloved connecting intimately with another man.

From there I had a string of relationships in which I mostly suppressed my desire to connect outside of my partnership. This withholding strategy didn't work, as most of these relationships ended with them falling madly in love with me, not realizing I was suppressing a big part of me. They were heartbroken over the loss of a woman they never truly knew. So then I went to the other end of the spectrum. During a hoe phase and BDSM exploration chapter in my early twenties, I convinced a man 24 years my senior to open-relate with me. He turned out to be a compulsive liar and would disappear for days with other women. It scared me away from open-relating for a while. So many of us try polyamory and end up burnt because we don't have the tools to do it effectively.

It's also confusing because there are so few accessible and successful examples of polyamorous couples. When I invite others to consider open-relating, they often immediately dismiss the idea, saying, "I don't know of any open relationship that has ended well." And I see where they're coming from, but with the current divorce rates where they are, we can't claim that monogamy and traditional life partnership is foolproof either. Approximately 40-50% of first marriages end in divorce, according to the American Psychological Association. For second marriages, that number soars to a divorce rate of 60-67%. I want to be clear, I don't measure the success of a partnership by longevity, but if commitment is the intention, it's clear the current societally acceptable relating structure is missing the mark. I don't think open-relating is the answer for everyone, but maybe it's worth exploring.

HOW TO HAVE IT ALL

I have totally bought into the societally and anatomically perpetuated feminine vision of being a wife and mother. It's something I always dreamed of since I was a little girl with my baby dolls. At 5 years old, I'd lie in bed pretending my future husband was there with me on the other side of my Cabbage Patch Kid. I ached for him, as I ached for a traditional family structure. With my parents divorced since I was 3 and very much emotionally unavailable, I longed for love and touch and a *normal* family. I was looking for my *perfect match* in kindergarten. And I never stopped until the year I met my husband. To be clear, I'm not saying *he* ended the search – I did when I decided to get really clear on where my desire for life partnership was coming from. **It took disentangling my true desire for life partnership from my conditioning.** It took getting curious about why I wanted a husband and family, other than the fact I'd been spoon-fed visuals of happily-ever-after since I was a toddler. It took immense heartbreak.

Originally I held the vision of spending my life with the man I dated the year prior to meeting my husband. We loved each other. He would've been a great father. We both felt ready for that chapter. And yet, we ended the relationship before the rest of our lives began. Part of our breakup was my own lack of faithfulness, which I shared in previous chapters. I didn't trust him to stay, but mostly, I didn't trust myself to be able to uphold the more traditional values he carried. It was this incompatibility, along with my own ignorance of my deeper desire, that led me to emotionally cheat (and toe the line of physical cheating). I finally came to the conclusion that I just wasn't cut out for traditional monogamy. And I needed someone who was very secure in their belief of the same. But it also led me to consider whether I was cut out for deep commitment at all. I knew I wanted a life partner, but I wasn't clear on if that desire was a reflection of my highest truth OR of the conditioning I experienced, which very much boxes us into lifetime commitment to one person.

After our breakup, I was tempted to immediately go on the prowl for the next bigger and better candidate to life partnership. I had to intentionally and consciously slooooow down. It wasn't just the loss of the man I loved creating so much grief post-breakup; it was also the loss of the vision we had together. It was the loss of the home and family I *almost* had. The heartache was debilitating and depressing. I lost 10 pounds and my sanity.

On the other side, I knew I was unavailable for that kind of heartbreak to happen ever again. And to prevent that, I had to let die what I knew and be reborn in the possibility of my deepest desire. I had to get really clear on what I wanted and dream outside of what I had evidence for. I went back into the dating world with the intention of exploring different relating styles and different types of men to gain clarity for what I wanted in a partnership.

I came out the other side realizing *I wanted it all*. I had always wanted it all. I wanted the deep commitment that brings life partnership, a shared home, and a core family unit. But I also wanted the freedom to explore all of my humanity, my pleasures, and my darkest desires. A traditional monogamous relationship wouldn't do, but neither would an incredibly open and polyamorous partnership. In fact, I wasn't convinced there was ONE relating style I could commit to for the rest of my life. And despite being heavily involved in conscious, open-minded, and kink-friendly communities, I didn't know of a single relationship that I desired to replicate for myself. There were several that had qualities I admired, but none I wanted holistically. So I came to the conclusion that what I desired was either not possible (meaning I would continue to sacrifice what I wanted deep down) OR it just hadn't been done yet or shared openly, and it was my duty to become evidence of what is possible. I decided to give it six months. If I couldn't intentionally create my dream relationship of commitment and freedom in that time frame (or at least create some evidence of its possibility), I'd head back to the drawing board. I wrote down all the qualities I desired in my life partner, including celebrating and supporting my seemingly contradictory desires.

Just over two weeks later, at a gathering amongst friends, Andrew and I fell in love. Despite my deep soul yearning and the blooming passion, I wrote off the potential of us becoming anything, especially life partners. I judged him on the surface as incompatible with my vision. He presents quite traditional; I had been-there-done-that and wasn't trying to go back. And yet... we did meet at one of my sacred sex events... and the attraction was undeniable. I agreed to a first date, which happened to be a Tantra play party. Our clothes stayed on and we didn't even kiss until we came back to my apartment. It was the best first kiss of my life – and he felt it too. When he led me into my bedroom, it wasn't to take off my clothes, it was to undress in vulnerability. He invited me to be naked in my highest truth and grandest soul expression. He asked me what I *really* wanted. What I *really, really* wanted. I leaned in with trust to the holy contradiction of risk and reward. Pushing my ego to the back seat, with my journal in my hands like a prayer book, I straddled his torso and read aloud the entry detailing my ideal life partnership.

"I'm going to marry you." Then and there, on our first date, Andrew said he would marry me. I fell over, giggling in a nervous surrender as he continued... *I didn't think a woman existed that wanted* all *that... I didn't know that type of relationship was possible.* Neither did I, but I asked him if he wanted to create it with me. I asked him if he wanted our relationship to be the example of a new way of relating, if we could be evidence of what is possible.

That night we committed to each other and agreed our relationship wouldn't be defined by a relating structure. In each season of life we would consider what relating style would support our greatest opportunities for growth and expansion. Thus far, there have been chapters that have felt very open and others that have felt more monogamous. I trust there will be forthcoming seasons with even more supplementary lovers and others that feel radically closed to outer connections. And throughout it all, our one constant has been *out is not an option*. We are wildly committed to one another, and all outside connections must be at least net-neutral to our primary partnership, if not net-positive.

We define net-positive connections as those that bring us closer to our highest selves and each other. This is very subjective and is reliant on the current state of the relationship and the state of mind of both individuals in the partnership. The same exact external intimate act and secondary partner could appear net-positive one day and net-negative the next. It takes conscious **compersion, curiosity,** and **nourishment** to lean into the net-positive benefits of secondary partners.

Compersion is defined as *vicarious joy associated with seeing one's partner have a joyful romantic or sexual relation with another.* When we can celebrate our partner's external love or pleasure, we are in net-positive territory, because both partners feel the good-feels. For example, I have witnessed Andrew receive the most glorious lingam massage during a workshop, and it brought me to tears witnessing the devotion this woman offered the love of my life.

Curiosity allows us to consider benefits of external connections that may be easily overlooked when we are projecting patterns or stories into the mix. It is so easy to get jealous when our partner comes home from a lover all aglow. But what if the love they co-created with another filled them up so they are overflowing back onto you? What if their new lover introduced them to a new sex trick, way of being, or communication tool that may inspire deeper connection in your own partnership? Andrew once came back from connecting with a woman, boasting of how well he held her, detailing the safety and healing he made space for. How he inspired her catharsis and revelation of desires. My immediate reaction was to feel threatened. I shared this with Andrew and he held me through it. Soon after, I began to get curious about how his experience in holding this woman had inspired him to claim his gift as a shamanic healer. This translated to recognizing his confidence in holding me and co-facilitating would both be amplified.

To receive the gifts of compersion and curiosity, it is best to be **well-nourished**. This means our relationship to each other is nourished, and as individuals we are nourishing ourselves. Before either of us facilitate or attend a play party, retreat, sexy event, or Tantra festival, Andrew and I make sure to set aside a few hours of intimacy, just the two of us. This way we go into our events overflowing in love for each other, rather than desperately seeking attention wherever we can find it.

As for individual nourishment, Andrew and I have achieved this by making God our first priority, then our relationship. Godliness is a part of me – my God is my higher self and my grander purpose. When I prioritize godliness, I treat myself as sacred. I eat well, move my body, get enough sleep, and do all the self-care things I need to be nourished.

One time I felt so undernourished, tired, and out of sync, I consented to Andrew connecting with another woman just because I knew I had nothing to give. That was a learning moment, because from this undernourished space it is much harder to experience compersion and curiosity. When you are undernourished, you are in survival mode, making it much more difficult to think critically. While Andrew was out with another woman, I ended up spending the night spiraling in the unknowns, anxious and awake rather than getting the sleep I very much needed. After that experience, we agreed to not make any decisions about external connections unless we were both fully nourished physically and in the relationship.

RELATIONAL STRUCTURES DEFINED AND LIBERATED

Relating structures come in all shapes and colors, and are totally customizable to your relationship preferences, desires, boundaries, and needs for safety. The range of open-relating vs. monogamy may be categorized by sexual exclusivity (or the lack thereof) AND emotional exclusivity (or the lack thereof). Jessica Fern's book Polysecure is one of the best resources I've come across in approaching any level of ethical non-monogamy safely. On the next page you will find a chart exemplifying the most common labels for relating structures and how they compare in terms of sexual and emotional exclusivity: Here are some brief definitions of these relating styles with their typical agreements:

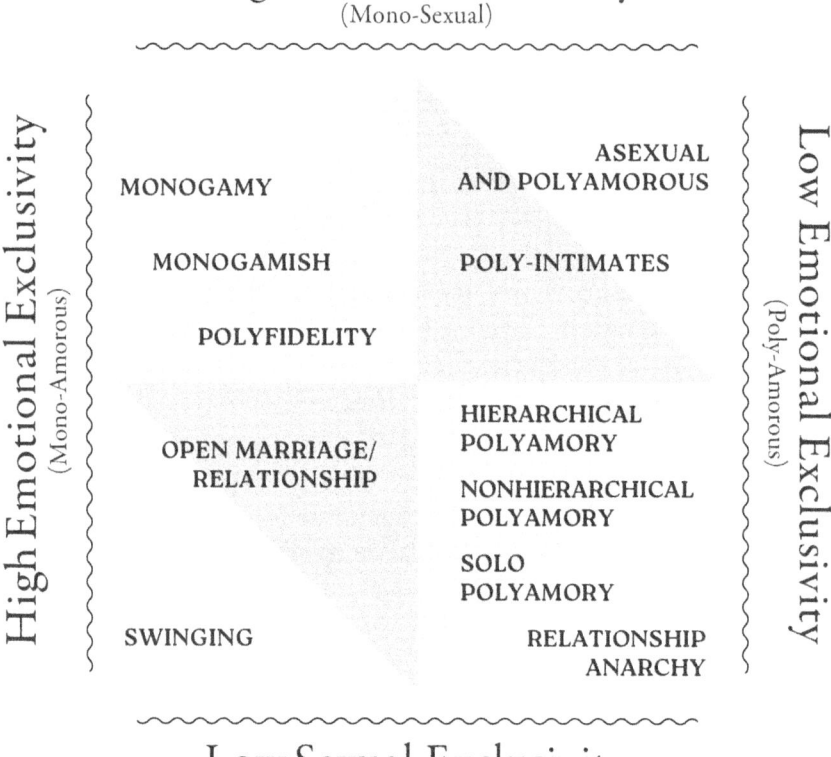

RELATING STYLES
Based on Jessica Fern's chart of the types of non-monogamy

Monogamy: the practice of having a sexual relationship (or marriage) with one person at a time

Monogamish: first coined by Dan Savage, an American journalist, author, and columnist, to describe long-term committed partnership, with occasional intimate encounters with other people, or an interest in such

Polyfidelity: all partners in a group agree not to have romantic and sexual relationships outside the established group

Open Marriage/Relationship: involves sexual relations with multiple people, in and outside the partnership

Swinging: couples "swap" sexual partners

Asexual Polyamory: usually involves an asexual individual who has a single partner, in which one or both partners has outside partnerships, which are usually more sexually exclusive

Poly-Intimates: usually involves sexual exclusivity with one person, but creates space for emotional and/or platonic external relationships of elevated importance or shared resource

Hierarchical Polyamory: open-relating involving other partners, but one or more partners is prioritized OR has a greater level of commitment than secondary partners

Nonhierarchical Polyamory: open-relating involving multiple partners where all relationship pairs are treated equally and as separate entities

Solo Polyamory: individuals connect sexually with others, but do not couple and focus on relationship to oneself

Relationship Anarchy: no definable structure, fluid with no solid differentiation between sexual, romantic, or platonic relationships

All the above are *brief* definitions and may be adapted from person to person and relationship to relationship. Relationship styles are just as variable as the humans in them!

HOW TO CHOOSE THE RIGHT RELATING STYLE FOR YOU

At the end of the day, as with all other considerations in Tantra, there is no *right* or *wrong* relating style. It's all about intention. Both polyamory and monogamy have the capability to support expansion and liberation... and they can both be a crutch for limitation and fear.

Monogamy can be intentionally evoked for expansion when we choose this type of commitment with the desire to go really deep with one person – to claim a partner in exploration of the possibilities that alight when we focus and use our partner as a mirror for mutual growth and ascension. Contrary to popular belief, monogamy is not the end of freedom. It is the end of a particular variety, but it is the beginning of a new era of emotional freedom, depth, and ability to potentially create something much bigger with another than you could create alone. It can be a 1+1=3 equation.

Monogamy *can* be limiting when it is chosen from fear. I believe a majority of monogamous couples choose monogamy with at least a bit of fear that their partner will leave them if they open the relationship. Monogamy appears "easier" to many of us, so we choose it to keep things simple. Yet, it can also perpetuate co-dependency and anxious attachment patterns. Often a fear-based intention can live alongside an expansive intention. A couple may choose monogamy to go really deep in the commitment AND have fear of potential abandonment that can come from opening up. *It's often not either/or, it's both and MORE.*

Polyamory and other forms of non-monogamy have an inverse and parallel potential for intentionality. Some choose polyamory from the expansive intention of celebrating all the love they have to give and explore. They desire the freedom to express their range of intimacy with anyone they feel called to on their path, and they recognize committed partnership to be a barrier for this type of liberation.

Alternatively, they may be choosing non-monogamy out of fear of commitment; they may be perpetuating an avoidant attachment pattern. As with monogamy, it's just as likely for someone choosing polyamory to have shades of expansive intention alongside lingering fear-based intentions.

Ethical non-monogamy has the fun-comfortable result of enhancing the foundations of the relationship. It tends to amplify joy and connectedness in relationships which already have a solid foundation. But if a relationship has a rocky foundation, non-monogamy will often rock the relationship. It brings to the surface concerns that would be hidden in the ease and simplicity of monogamy. Jealousy, insecurities, shadows, fears, and limiting patterns have nowhere to hide and are consistently triggered to the surface. Open-relating requires us to own our triggers and pleasures to a greater extent and at a faster rate than we could imagine in monogamy. It can collapse timelines for breakdowns and potential breakthroughs. Non-monogamy has the potential power to catapult us into self-awareness and growth at a much faster rate than monogamy, but it comes with a greater risk and responsibility.

I find it to be most expansive to consider what relating style offers the greatest opportunity for growth *for you* (and your potential partner, if it applies) *in this moment.* Give yourself grace to change your mind; you are not required to marry a relating style. While Andrew and I spent the first year of our relationship with some degree of openness, when it came time to get married, we felt called to a more monogamous structure. Focusing on each other, our bond, and our foundations at this critical time of lifetime commitment felt *just right* for the initiation of marriage. We have since exhaled into more openness once more. We are in consistent curiosity, changing our relating structure on a whim as it supports the higher good of our relationship.

I learned so much about the breadth of relating styles by experimenting with them and trusting my body to clue me into what worked for me for each partnership. Frank Mondeose, founder of *Love Without Limit*, also known as "The Spiritual Playboy," calls this finding *right* relationship. *Right* relationship involves letting go of our egoic desires and expectations for how a relationship will play out and be defined in its relating structure. When meeting potential lovers, we often put them into a box, usually labeled *potentially the one* or *just for fun*. Doing so keeps us from living in the present potential. It keeps us projecting our past experiences and societal expectations onto the relationship, rather than getting curious about possibilities for co-creation that may be *just right*.

Frank is an advocate for *love without limit.* This seemingly idealistic perspective of love is simply defined by our ability to support, contribute, and celebrate the expansion of the beloved. *Love without limit* allows us to release our concept of what is *best* for our partner, and instead love them unconditionally, even when their choices don't align with our desires. Regardless of your relating style, *love without limit* is within reach. For more on how to achieve *love without limit,* see the resources section at the end of this book to find his website and other related works.

This chapter is just the tip of the iceberg in understanding and providing context for the broad spectrum of relating styles. There's so much space to create safety within your partnerships which support your unique definitions of love, expansion, and liberation.

HOMEPLAY
Sacred Sex Ed integration activities and expansive opportunities to transform the way you make love to life.

CORD CUTTING RITUAL
Supplies: meditation music and your imagination

Relationships shouldn't hold you back. They should set you free. Free to unlock your greatest potential and highest self, with the support and celebration of a loving and compatible partner. But societal conditionings, unhealthy attachments, co-dependency, and past trauma creates fears that take the shape of weighty cords.

Performing a cord cutting ritual or meditation supports you in letting go of what is no longer serving the relationship, unlocking potential to grow together in new expansive ways. This is a great practice to do with a current partner in mind OR to release a relationship that is no longer serving you.

1. Put on some gentle meditation music or step outside into the organic sounds of nature. Consider using a guided cord cutting meditation – one can be found on the *Talk Tantra to Me* Podcast, episode 37: https://www.talktantratome.com/podcast

2. After relaxing your body and dropping in, call forth the energy of your higher self.

3. Imagine the other person standing in front of you. Visualize weighty, chain-like cords between you, as well as light cords that appear as beams of light. These cords may be connected at each of the seven chakra points, or between the hearts or sex of both individuals.

4. Consider the "meaning" between the cords, even drawing evidence from your relationship to demonstrate which are "heavy" and which are "light."

5. Now imagine you have a large sword that slices through the weighty cords, while keeping the light cords intact. Say aloud, "*I am free. You are free.*"

6. Continue slicing through each of the weighty cords until you are liberated.

7. Consider what (if any) integration steps need to be taken to anchor in this work. This may mean setting boundaries, having clearing conversations, or setting intentions.

PART 3

Liberate Your Eros

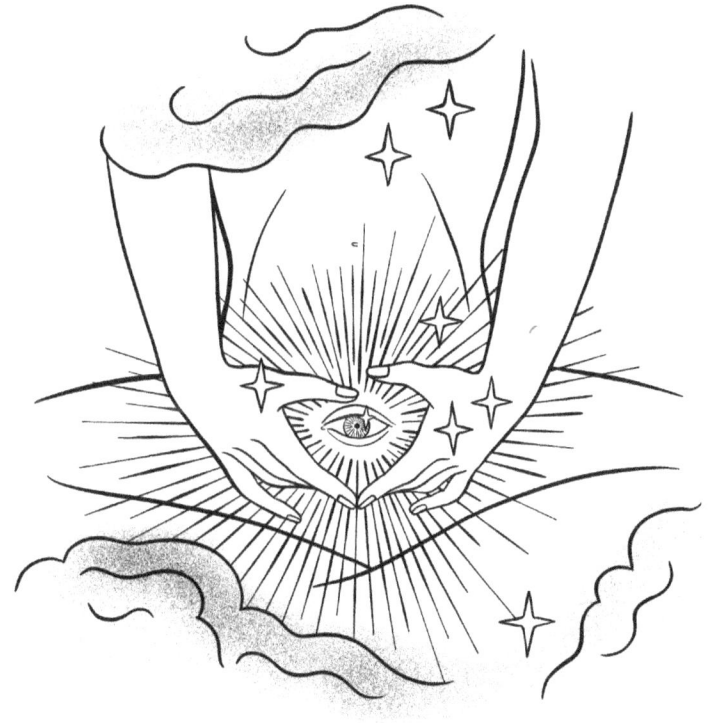

CHAPTER 11:

DISCOVER YOUR GOLDEN SHADOW

As we've learned in previous chapters, we are often unconsciously avoiding and projecting the deeper parts of ourselves, our psyches, and our conditionings. When we hide the parts of ourselves we don't want others to see, we live in the dark. Our darkness can seem scary, and, in many cases, inherently bad. But there's a lot of beauty that happens in our metaphorical darkness. The dark is primal, magical, and transformative. It is in the darkness of the womb that a baby is grown; it is in the darkness of the chrysalis that a caterpillar becomes a butterfly; it is in the darkness of soil that a seed sprouts.

Many spiritual communities perpetuate ignorance of the dark, touting "love" and "light." I assure you there is just as much love for you in the dark – it is only demonized for its raw and primal truth. And there is just as much distortion and "shadowy" behavior in communities of "light" – consider televangelists who misappropriate funds, the Crusades which killed an estimated one million innocent people between 1096 and 1291, or countless Catholic priests accused of raping children.

In this chapter, we're going to go deeper into what we may be missing in the ignorance of our darkness. We've already deeply explored the concept of shadow work and how it relates to our intimate lives. Much of the shadow work we've addressed thus far has to do with healing deeply rooted limiting beliefs, shame, guilt, and fear around sexuality and our bodies imposed by society and institutions. We're aware of the shadowy distortions that have ruled our perspective, but there's a whole other side to our shadow that is bright, shiny, and fun!

The Golden Shadow is a gift within you that you've unconsciously hidden as a way to protect yourself from unwanted attention or perceived potential negative consequences. Shadow work, the concept of integrating parts of ourselves which we've denied or disowned, can be laborious, feel endless, and lead to a lot of emotional release. And yet, on the other side of shadow work, there's a juiciness and liberation which gets to be celebrated. The golden shadow represents elements of our purpose or medicine for the world that we're not sharing – *it is untapped potential or unexplored possibilities for pleasure.*

For example, you may have an incredible talent for music. You love music and you're naturally amazing at harmonizing and inventing tunes. But you never sing. You never play instruments. You never explore this side of yourself. *Why?* Because when you play music, you get lots of attention. And that means you are the center of attention, which is super vulnerable and feels unsafe. You may have even previously been super comfortable exploring this gift, singing loud and proud, but were chastised for being too loud or off pitch... and that one criticism stuck with you and created the belief that it is safer to play small and be unseen to avoid potential judgment.

In cases such as this, it is common for the individual with the golden shadow to get close to others who share a similar gift, which they are suppressing. For example, those who desire to be artists, and may even have a true talent for it, become art collectors or dealers; those with a talent for writing end up editing the works of others, etc. It appears safer to be in the circle of their passion passively than to be naked in the vulnerability of being seen pursuing their authentic self.

This fear of judgment from our peers, family, or society can keep us from executing our soul purpose. For years, I skirted around my very obvious gifts of sensuality, self-love, and sexual healing. My tantrika codes were so very deeply buried in my golden shadow that even when I had people tell me I should pursue Tantra as a career, I completely disregarded them. It took one very devoted individual shining light on my golden shadow and creating evidence of what I was capable of. Then I finally began dipping my toes into the potential of sharing this gift with the world.

From there, it still took me a whole year before I talked about my work publicly. In the beginning, my services were very much on the down-low. When I first started healing others using sacred intimacy, I was terrified to tell the people closest to me, let alone my social media following. My conditioning of shame and guilt around sex and exchanging money for my soul purpose was still very debilitating, even though I witnessed countless times from personal experience and with clients how incredibly healing working with your sexuality can be. Eventually, I started talking about it with friends and family, but I was very clear to say it wasn't sex work... And how I work with individuals is definitely NOT sex work *in a traditional sense*.

But it is sexual, healing, and very expansive. And it is my duty to share this with the world. I inevitably got over the fear-induced secrecy in regard to my work when the mounting evidence of how transformative Tantra and sacred sexuality can be outweighed my own worries of judgment and ridicule. Eventually, I realized it was my duty to share this gift – to show up with purpose and share my truth to inspire and awaken others. I've come so far as to reclaim the meaning of sex work. Times are changing. Systems are crumbling.

Writing this book *is* sex work. The future of sex work is much bigger than exchanging money to masturbate with someone's body. It's using our inherent innocence, Eros, and sexuality to expand collective consciousness and heal the planet. Everything in this book is what sex work looks like as we transcend into higher states of consciousness. We're removing the shame and guilt while living in our highest love and truth. This allows us to heal our sexual trauma instead of repeating the patterns that keep us intimately blocked.

The world needs individuals living in the fullness of their presence, pleasure, and purpose. This is less about becoming a teacher or guru and more about being the embodiment of a sexually liberated human. It means becoming turned on by life. It means using the tools in this book, being intentional intimately, being naked in your vulnerability, and consciously communicating your desires. The ability to move through the world with that kind of self-awareness and self-love is golden. This can be as simple as just practicing and integrating what you've learned about yourself in reading this book – I promise *that alone is enough* to inspire the people around you and become evidence of what is possible.

Or you may find yourself motivated to alchemize your mess into your medicine, dedicating your life to bringing the wisdom that worked for you into your own community. If you're like me, you might have felt this calling but struggled to fully step into your potential. My inner critic reared its head (and still does!), leading me to stifle my voice, my magic, and my medicine. *The world doesn't need another Tantra coach. There's already thousands out there. Everyone already knows this stuff... it's obvious. Who am I to pretend I know anything about anything?* But I did it anyway. Because **there will not be enough Tantra coaches, therapists, energy healers, medicine shamans, life coaches, or self-development professionals of any variety until this planet is free of sexual assault, violence is non-existent, and everyone is truly turned on by life.**

By those metrics, we have a long way to go and we need a lot more individuals on the front lines spreading the message of divine love. So if you feel any part of yourself resistant to stepping into your passion and purpose, I beg you to *do it anyways*. We need your gifts. We need your light. We need as many awakened and expansive souls as possible to step into leadership – to create evidence of new Earth in their lives, relationships, AND businesses. Your unique story and lived experiences have a way of relating to your own community that no one else has. There are people in your immediate circle that need your golden shadow; that need you to be evidence of what is possible for them. **The best thing you can do for the people in your life is be your most authentic self**, which involves integrating all that you are – shadows, darkness, and light! This is your sign to do the thing, that thing that you feel like you're not worthy of doing or that you're scared of doing. It may be your key to finding the meaning of your life, to making an impact and creating wealth, or to meeting true love. I wouldn't have any of these things if I hadn't honored my authentic self. The greatest outcome of all is evident in my relationships.

LOVE YOURSELF AND THE WORLD WILL LOVE YOU TOO

I wouldn't have met the love of my life, Andrew, if I hadn't integrated my golden shadow. We wouldn't have fallen in love if I hadn't done years of shadow work to excavate my authentic self and my authentic desires. For decades, I bypassed what I really wanted from love and relationships to protect myself from judgment, rejection, and abandonment. When someone expressed interest in me, I often contorted myself into who they desired me to be and prioritized the relational structure they desired, instead of

CHAPTER 11: DISCOVER YOUR GOLDEN SHADOW

sharing what I really wanted. In many ways I didn't even know what kind of relationship I wanted because I was too terrified of shining light on those subconscious desires and finding something outside the bounds of societal norms.

This became harder to do as I stepped into my purpose as a pleasure priestess (see more on what being a pleasure priestess entails in chapter 15). Even then, I felt like I had to rationalize my work and over-explain myself to make my partners comfortable. I had to make them understand who I was and what I did, rather than trusting my magic to shine through inherently. I will say, being more forthright about my profession became a very effective dating filter. Being a sexually liberated woman intimidates most men, so anyone not up for the initiation of dating someone like me usually makes a hasty exit. I could take this personally, but I decided early on to see it as a blessing – less time wasted, more real relating. And yet, I have still feared my dates would judge my work, misunderstand me, or misconstrue my expansive intentions. Deep down, a part of me felt *too difficult to date... too wild... too autonomous... too unconventional. No man would ever commit to a woman like me.* So I settled in relationships that didn't fully light my fire and I made myself smaller to appear easier, tamer, and more conventional.

I was unconsciously sabotaging myself, hurting these men, and wasting everyone's time. *Ouch* – a hard pill to swallow. That's shadow work for you. But even in this realization, there was a big, shiny golden nugget. I am a pleasure priestess. The parts of me that I deemed "challenging" are actually what make me most lovable to the partners who are actually FOR ME. My perspective on love and sex makes me *more* lovable. I am worthy of being put on a pedestal and chosen by an amazing man *because* of my unique magic. I can help my partners see their body in a new light, set their passions ablaze, and give them the tools to have the best sex of their life. There is a line of men outside the door waiting to date that kind of woman; *waiting to date me*!

It is often the parts of ourselves that feel the most self-conscious, shameful, or wounded that hold our greatest opportunity for stepping into our purpose. *Your pain becomes your purpose; your mess becomes your medicine.* Consider flipping the script on your "faults" or "regrets" – they could actually be your greatest blessings in disguise. I deeply resented the sexual parts of me, believing you can't be sexual AND successful. You can't be sexual

AND spiritual. Those things just didn't go together in the narrative I was raised with. But the more awareness and attention I gave these parts of myself, the more I integrated into my true self, leading to a whole-lotta-self-love.

I stepped up and into my purpose… and received an abundantly rewarding career, a loving and open-minded community, and the love of my life! Andrew and I met at a Tantra workshop I was facilitating. We literally wouldn't have even been in the same room if it weren't for me allowing my golden shadow to shine. He wouldn't have witnessed the divinely powerful woman I am if I hadn't stepped up as a leader. He saw me for who I was – pleasure priestess and all – and loved me for it, because I was being my full authentic self. Interestingly, in those early days of the relationship, I helped Andrew retrieve a bit of his golden shadow.

FINDING GOD IN THE DARK

When Andrew and I met, I saw something most people were missing. He had a superpower that I don't even think he fully saw or had claimed. I started calling him a Dark Wizard. Andrew resented this in the beginning, but he now loves and owns this part of himself. To me, a Dark Wizard is the male equivalent of a witch – deeply primal and powerful. I, being the intuitive feminine oracle I am, saw in Andrew an enormous amount of power. A power to lead, and also a power to manipulate.

To be *manipulative* is generally considered dangerous or toxic. However, one definition of *manipulate* is *to influence cleverly*. This is *so* Andrew – he is incredibly skilled with communication and emotional intelligence to influence people. With courage, this power can be channeled for the greater good, especially when it is owned and consciously wielded. And it can be messy, and even dangerous, when used unconsciously.

Consider Batman or Severus Snape – both prime examples of Dark Wizards and master manipulators. Spoiler alert: Throughout the entire *Harry Potter* saga, Snape is made out to be a sort of villain. By book six, he is revealed as a Death Eater, Lord Voldemort's right-hand man, and murderer of the beloved Dumbledore. By the end of the final and seventh book, it is revealed that all along, Snape was using his Dark Wizard powers to manipulate Voldemort – he was secretly helping Harry. He managed to fool one of the most dangerous and powerful wizards in history for the greater good of all and out of the deepest love. This is a unique skillset – to manipulate and lie, literally to save lives. No Gryffindor, such as myself, would be able to do it. But Andrew, a Slytherin through and through, most certainly could. This is what we're capable of when we reclaim the parts of ourselves that we've been conditioned to believe are "bad." We're able to use them as assets consciously and avoid projecting them in unhealthy ways. I wonder what would have happened if Voldemort had been truly loved and taught to wield his Dark Wizardry with such reverence?

My beautiful darkness looks a little different. I am a sacred rebel. Being a rebel doesn't necessarily mean acting out – my rebel is purely a part of my existence. Just by being myself, I am contradicting the common narrative, and therefore rebelling. I love this part of myself – the highly discerning archetype within me that is willing to stand in her truth at all costs. Even when it means upsetting others. But as with all archetypes, there is a shadow, one I unconsciously allowed to create drama in my life. Being a rebel comes with consequences. I am usually able to hold those consequences, meaning when I trigger a reaction from someone else, I don't take on their projection. I know who I am and am firm in my foundations.

But before my sacred rebel was fully integrated, I let the consequences of my inner rebel shake me to my core and throw salt in a wound I'd been neglecting. During a leadership training, I stood as a source for a new style of leadership, one that advocated for flow and ease. While the training pushed for more action and urgency, I did the opposite, focusing on being magnetic and creating spaciousness for time off. Despite my "different" way of doing things, I was excelling in all the metrics they gave us to determine successful leadership. However, I was chastised in front of my peers for stepping outside their definition of leadership and was unceremoniously demoted. A part of me was flabbergasted – I was completely naive to the potential consequences of my eccentricity. And a part of me was totally turned on by the drama I had created for myself and others. It was an existential kink alight within me.

While I have no regrets for asserting my values, there was a learning lesson here. My naivety revealed a secret penchant for creating a bit of chaos in the name of progress (channeling my inner Tantra Goddess Kali – she who creates and destroys worlds). And yet, the consequences of public denunciation left me vulnerable to the inevitable tarnishing of my ego. I let the reaction of others make me "bad" and "wrong." I literally questioned my identity and my worth, swinging on a pendulum between self-righteousness and self-deprecation. It was a death spiral, leading me directly to an unhealed part of myself I got to make love to and integrate.

That's the thing: **Even when your inner rebel (or any other golden archetypal shadow within you) is "true," that doesn't mean they are mature.** They don't get the driver's seat (at least not by default). They get to consciously be seen, heard, and loved because if they are not expressed, they will make themselves known. And we may or may not be prepared for the consequences. As I've consciously integrated my inner rebel, I've fallen deeper in love with her. I have such reverence for her courage and destruction. I've created space for her to "act out" and find herself. This is the process of "growing up" – meeting our shadow with love, patience, and alchemy.

When we give ourselves permission to explore our darkest desires, hidden powers, and primal pulses, we make love to our life force energy. *We have more of ourselves to play with* for greater presence, more fulfilling pleasure, and purposeful relating.

HOMEPLAY
Sacred Sex Ed integration activities and expansive opportunities to transform the way you make love to life.

RECOVERING YOUR GOLDEN SHADOW
Supplies: pen, paper, and your imagination!

Find a quiet space to be introspective with your journal.

1. Bring forth the energies of envy and jealousy. What experiences, people, or concepts bring forth these feelings? What might they say about your own desires?

2. Who do you idolize or put on a pedestal? What might that reveal about who you desire to be in this world?

3. Call forth your inner critic or the part of you that feels like an imposter. How could their fears be keeping you from your magic? What are they trying to protect? What do they want you to hear before moving forward?

4. Consider your "faults" and "imperfections." How could these perceived weaknesses be channeled or alchemized into superpowers?

5. Take a moment to be with these answers and observe any synchronicities that could be illuminating.

CHAPTER 12:

SEX MAGIC 101

I will never underestimate the power of getting clear on my deepest desires and masturbating about it. This is sex magic. The intention is to harness life force energy to create opportunities and experiences that your soul craves. I credit sex magic to manifesting my dream man, dream car, dream job; all dreams come true when I cum.

The concept of sex magic is supported by the Law of Attraction. This energetic principle relies on the belief that all things are energy and that like energies attract one another. *As above, so below.* When you think positively (gratitude, pleasure, trust, etc.), you are a magnet for more positive opportunities and experiences. On the other hand, negative thinking and lower frequencies (fear, shame, guilt, etc.) create more "negative" circumstances. The more you victimize yourself or wallow, the more you likely you are to perceive your experiences as something to feel powerless over.

That being said, it is very important to fully feel, heal, and integrate traumatic experiences and triggers. Bypassing low-vibe experiences and emotions is just as ineffective as wallowing or perpetuating a victim mindset. I used to be a serial bypasser, meaning I was constantly bottling up my emotions and minimizing my trauma. Being a victim made me feel so out of control that I didn't even allow myself to process and grieve experiences as intense as sexual assault.

When I woke up to a man penetrating my ass after a night out drinking in college, I told my friend I had wanted it. This was so far from the truth, but it was easier for me to lie to myself and my friend than it was for me to come to terms with rape. I spent six years projecting this trauma into my life and avoiding anything close to anal sex, until I began practicing anal de-armoring on myself and processing what happened with a sex coach. Finally, I didn't get triggered whenever a guy tried to do doggy style. Finally, I could touch my own butt and feel pleasure instead of disgust. This is the sexual shadow work piece. It's very important to continue to do the messy processing and healing to truly be effective in sex magic and become a pleasure priest or priestess.

Having a positive mindset does not make you immune to unfortunate events, triggers, or trauma. It's about *being an alchemist.* Even in the face of the most difficult or backwards circumstances, you are able to come back to the result of feeling empowered to co-create your reality with your highest self and divine support by your side. This is about *choosing* how to respond to triggers, rather than reacting based on past trauma, limiting beliefs, or conditionings. You get to decide if you'd like upsets to ruin your day (or life!) or whether you can process your feelings, find a silver lining, and move on.

When you groggily get up and realize you're out of coffee, you can either get mad at your roommate for forgetting to buy more OR you can take it as a sign that maybe your body needs the purifying elements of green tea instead. When you survive a life-altering trauma, you can decide to get angry at our creator for bringing you into such a violent and sad world OR you can use it as motivation to start living your life! This perspective is shared immaculately in the cult classic book The Secret by Rhonda Byrne and is backed up by science in *Becoming Supernatural* by Dr. Joe Dispenza.

But what does this have to do with your sex life?

When do you feel the most ecstatic? When do you feel the most pleasure? When do you feel the most connected to something outside of yourself? When do you feel like your most divine self? For many, including myself, it's at the height of sexual pleasure. When I'm turned on, I feel *turned on* to the infinite potential of life. As we've explored in previous chapters, pleasure and climax can be seen as an altered and expansive state of consciousness. We get high on our own supply of life force and may feel capable of anything. Of course, many of us struggle to fully surrender to this limitlessness, as we have a racket of conditionings, past traumas, and limiting beliefs floating through our consciousness. Again, this is why it is *so* important to work through your sexual shadow – healing could even be the intention of your sex magic ritual!

When we intentionally tap into our orgasmic life force energy, we become an incredibly strong magnet for more goodness or ecstasy to come into our lives. The energy that we tap into with sexual pleasure is called life force energy (also commonly referred to as Eros or kundalini). It is powerful enough to create human life – babies are literally made as a result of sex. The first step to manifesting a child is arousal or "turn on," so life force is the catalyst to creating life. This is the energy that creates our entire reality. It seems to unfold totally naturally, as our creator intended. But what if you don't want to use the life force to make a breathing crying child? Where does that energy go? What else could you breathe life into?

What if you directed this energy into healing your physical body? Or calling in the love of your life? Or your dream home? Or building your business to make a greater impact and income? You could just cum. *But what if while you were cumming you visualized walking down the aisle… or getting the keys… or signing your dream client?* It's all about intention, baby. When we tap into our *turn on* with intention, we are aligning ourselves with an incredible creative force. By consciously calling forth your deepest desires at the heights of ecstasy through visualization, affirmation, and gratitude, you're anchoring them into our 3D world. During self-pleasure or partnered intimacy, you are able to harness pleasure and bliss to become a magnet for your desires using the Law of Attraction.

Mind blown. *Orgasm not included*

HERE ARE THE 7 STEPS TO SEX MAGIC

STEP 1: SET AN INTENTION.
What metaphorical "bun" do you want to put in the oven? Take some time to connect to your higher self and consider what you'd like to manifest. It could be a physical thing, like a car, money, or person. It could be more energetic, like the quality of healing or freedom. Consider journaling on

your vision for your life. Or create a vision board – a collage of images and words that represent your dream life. Allow this intention to find a home in your heart space... embody having it already. Get familiar with the visualizations, sensations, and affirmations that represent the thing you desire. My advice is to focus more on what kind of feeling you want to bring into your life, and less on the exact process or outcome.

For example, if you're looking to call in financial abundance, focus on what it would *feel* like to be financially secure and abundant. It doesn't hurt to also visualize a particular number in your bank account, but feeling is much stronger for anchoring it. If you're calling in sexual healing, consider the liberation and pleasure you may find on the other side.

As you practice, setting intentions will become easier and clearer. When I first started practicing sex magic, I was very vague and off-base with my intentions. For example, I'd ask for more "work" opportunities. Instead, a week later I got handed an unpaid writing project for an organization that freed children from sex trafficking. It was not at all what I intended, but that opportunity ended up being a catalyst for me stepping into sacred intimacy work professionally. In some ways it was a bit of an internship, providing me with experiences that demonstrated how important this work is for the world. (I share more about this "opportunity" and how it got me into this work in chapter 15.) In partnered intimacy, you can set intentions together. You could share things you desire to call in individually and as a couple. What would you like to co-create together? My husband and I have manifested our dream home, we've called in peace when there's been a lot of conflict between us, we've manifested a merging of purpose for greater impact, and we've called in promotions, as well as hundreds of thousands of dollars. I once had a partner who would have me list out what I was desiring to manifest as he began licking my pussy or making his first thrusts into my body. I called in community, rebirth, and love. He called in structure, land, and abundance. Every time we met, without fail, he'd ask, *"What are we calling in?"* His consistent leadership in harnessing our orgasmic potential literally changed the game for me. I now do not have self-pleasure or sex without setting an intention for directing my life force energy.

STEP 2: AWAKEN YOUR EROS.
Warm up the oven. Seduce yourself or each other with full presence and pleasure. Set the mood for this practice – light some candles and play some

mantras or meditation music. Take a nice bath or dance or have a glass of wine. Put on something luxurious and slip into clean sheets. Caress your body, or your lover's. Don't rush straight towards genitals. Move from your extremities – meaning the crown of the head, fingertips, and toes – inwards. Down the face, up the arms and legs, and finally to the pussy or penis. Take your time. The more you're able to build this energy, the stronger your life force becomes. Tease yourself and tease each other. Play with edging, bringing yourself to the brink of orgasm, and then slow down. *The more you are able to ride the orgasmic waves, the stronger a magnet you become to attract what you truly desire and deserve.*

STEP 3: MERGE INTENTION WITH LIFE FORCE AT CLIMAX.
Have the cake and eat it too. At each peak, bring your intention to mind. Visualize, with gratitude, receiving what you desire. Declare it out loud. *I am a millionaire. I am in love. I am changing the world!* Edging is powerful in this practice because it gives you multiple opportunities to anchor in your desires. Oftentimes the first time we practice sex magic, it can feel a bit unfamiliar, just like most things we have never done before. Give yourself grace and many opportunities to "practice" by bringing yourself to the edge of explosion and then backing off. You're also energetically expressing your commitment to the universe… by edging, you are declaring *I am willing to forgo immediate satisfaction to have what I really, really want in the long run. And I'm worthy of it.* It's like making an investment. Edging is giving the energy time to accrue before you cash out with the big O.

And when you finally do climax, *bask in it.* Visualize and sensationalize your intention and desires as if you are receiving them at that moment. A lot of us are in the pattern of immediately cleaning up, going on with our day, or having a sleep after orgasm. Disrupt this by staying in your pleasure and bliss as long as you can stand it. *Flex your receiving muscle* – revel in the visualization and affirmations of your manifestation. If you're practicing with a partner, spend time after sex to talk about your hopes, dreams, and vision for your relationship. If it feels approachable and palatable, consider anointing each other with your sexual fluids on your heart and third eye points. It's especially powerful to journal immediately after or share your visualizations with your partner to amplify the bliss of receiving. Connect to your intention as if it's already happened. Because, in some way, it already has. Time is a construct. There are various "potentials" for you to play out, and you have free will to choose which you want to experience by claiming your right as a conscious creator through the Law of Attraction.

STEP 4: INTEGRATE AND MAKE SPACE.
Let go of anything that isn't serving your intention. If you don't let go of limiting patterns and beliefs, you'll be sending mixed signals and you'll receive mixed results. For example, if you're manifesting a new partner, you need to cut the unhealthy ties with your ex. If you're calling in abundance, let go of the mindset and work opportunities that keep you stuck in survival mode.

STEP 5: BE GRATEFUL FOR ALL THAT YOU ALREADY HAVE.
Take a moment to consider the Earth has already so generously provided all your basic needs and so many desires without you ever really needing to make the *ask*. Consider how the stars have aligned, how fate has stepped in, how the universe has had your back to lead you to the human you are now... and to these wise words in front of you.

It is also absolutely essential that you first have gratitude for what you already have in your life to manifest more and better on an expedited timeline. Gratitude is the attitude of abundance. It is one of the highest frequencies of feeling, meaning it is a very effective vibration to use alongside the Law of Attraction. When we are grateful, we cannot dwell on what we don't have. Gratitude tells the universe, *Mmm, yummy, yes. More please!* If we focus on what we don't have, by the Law of Attraction, we will get more not-having-ness.

For example, as you manifest your dream vehicle, you might be angry at your old car for breaking down all the time. But if you can find some gratitude for how far this car has gotten you up until now, you'll be in a much better position to manifest something positive. When you are grateful to your ex for getting you closer to *the one,* you're not focused on getting revenge or wallowing in pity. Instead of lamenting over paying bills, say *thank you* with each payment – what a gift that you can afford rent, a car, and all those delightful charges on your credit card! The frequency of gratitude is much stronger than the frequency of anger or frustration.

STEP 6: TAKE ACTION.
Consider who you need to become to embody the manifestation you desire. If your intention is to call in abundance, how would an abundant person

be in the world? How would they treat money, opportunities, and people? If your intention is to call in love, how would a person in love act? They certainly wouldn't waste their time with people who are clearly not suitable. They would dress immaculately to impress their lover; they would see potential and beauty everywhere they looked.

The majority of sex magic is very feminine, surrendered, and in flow. But Tantra teaches us to find balance.

This is where the masculine *do-ing* comes in. Allow the feminine oracle to guide your inner masculine into action. If you're calling in abundance, create a new offering in your business, raise your prices, or put an ad online. If you're calling in healing, book an appointment with a health practitioner or read a book on a related subject matter. Allow yourself to be available to signs from the universe on how to move forward. Be prepared for your inner critic or imposter syndrome to come in, but trust that *you are supported to make big things happen in your life and in the world*. Use the tools of shadow work to move through your triggers and limiting beliefs with grace.

PERMISSION TO WANT WHAT YOU WANT

The day after I did a sex magic ritual to call in my life partner, I came across a flier at my local coffee shop. "Conscious Singles Speed Dating," it said in cheesy balloon font. *How pathetic. I wouldn't be caught dead at something like that. People that go to something like that must be* really *desperate*, I thought. I judged. And then I caught myself and got really curious. *Wow, this flier is really stirring something up inside of me.* I observed my emotional reactions without judgment. And decided I NEEDED to go to this event to confront my own fear-based, limiting beliefs. I found myself judging people that attend speed dating events as *desperate,* when in reality, most of them are probably just really committed to finding their life partner. So committed, in fact, that they're willing to put their heart on the line in front of a group of strangers. That's courageous.

I realized that deep down I was actually judging them for their desire, and, by extension, judging myself. After years of feminist conditioning that told me, "You don't need a man," and spiritual jargon that said all I needed was "self-love," I had taken on the belief that my desire to have life partnership was "wrong." I was not allowing myself to own the desire to have a life partner. I wasn't letting myself want what I wanted without shame. Maybe

I felt a little selfish for asking for what I wanted? Which brings me to my next point...

Allow yourself to want what you want. Sounds simple, right? Not so simple for those of us that have been taught to be selfless and to put others ahead of ourselves, to be people pleasers. Not so simple when we are fed an American Dream that often leaves us feeling *less than dreamy* – possibly dried up, tired, and uninspired? Not so simple when we're conditioned to believe going outside of the mold will lead to judgment, criticism, and even abandonment. Not so simple when we're told repeatedly that wealthy people are selfish, or doing what you love won't pay the bills, or freedom ends with marriage – or any other version of a scarcity mindset.

There is a divine reason why you want what you want. Give yourself permission to explore it. *What you desire, spirit desires for you. If this dream wasn't meant for you, it wouldn't be in your consciousness.* Spirit wants you to grow, to expand, to be able to receive more of all this life has to offer. Let go of the tendency to manifest based on what you have evidence for, what you've accomplished in the past, or what you've seen others accomplish. Allow yourself to dream beyond what is reasonable, beyond what feels achievable. Reach for the dream beyond your wildest imagination.

You may fear your desires come from ego – wanting to look good and feel cool. And maybe they are. However, the ego is not inherently bad. While I don't advise you to let your ego take the wheel, at least give it a seat in the car. **Make your ego an employee for your purpose.** Wanting a life partner may feel like an egoic desire. *How selfish of me to use my precious life force energy to manifest a husband when the world is in this state? Who am I to believe I deserve a life of love and commitment? No, I better manifest world peace instead.* But what if falling in love and raising compassionate, self-aware children has the ability to bring even more peace to the world than going to anti-war rallies and the like? Two people working towards the same cause is at least twice as effective. I like to say Sacred Union creates a 1+1=3 equation. Two whole individuals aligned intentionally have the capability to create something even bigger than themselves, literally and metaphorically.

CHAPTER 12: SEX MAGIC 101

I lived in LA for two years without a car – if you've spent any time in the city of angels, you'll agree I deserve some kind of medal. I joyously took the bus, rode my used bicycle, or splurged on the occasional Uber. I loved not having a car: the freedom from car payments, insurance, driving in traffic, never having to worry about parking or parking tickets. It felt expansive in that season of my life to be blissfully minimalistic. Then, suddenly, I craved a different kind of freedom. The kind of freedom that meant I could hop in my own chunk of metal at a whim and head towards the ocean on the west side of the city whenever I wanted. Also, my Tantra practice was expanding and calling me all over the city and into other, much farther corners of California. It felt like I was renting a car every other week. And let me tell ya, the waiting line at Budget Car Rental is far from liberating. So I decided it was time to manifest a car.

I buckled in for some sex magic, focusing entirely on the feeling of sitting in my car. I felt the leather steering wheel gliding under my palms and wind in my hair. *Yes, wind… mmm… a convertible will definitely make LA traffic more bearable. How can one have road rage with the top down?* I imagined myself driving to my appointments and out to the coast. Some would say the desire for a convertible is clearly egoic. It is a frivolous extra and I certainly didn't *need* it. *But what if my ego was on my side?* What if I allowed myself to want what I want? Wouldn't the joy of a convertible and wind beating against my open chest allow me to show up for my clients feeling fulfilled rather than frustrated about traffic on the way? If it makes me feel good, then my good feelings might just be infectious to everyone I meet! Even then, I imagined I'd end up in some twenty-year-old hunk of metal with a faded soft top and fringed holes, which would inevitably break down on one of my long road trips and likely need some kind of repair that basically doubled my costs in the long run. I couldn't fathom the idea of calling in a brand-new car.

But that's exactly what happened. With my budget of $5k, $6k max, I scoured Craigslist and even went to see a few used cars, one of which I put a deposit down for, but ended up not buying because it failed the inspection. I was beyond frustrated… until a dear friend asked me if I'd considered leasing. I hadn't and I didn't want to because I honestly didn't really know what it meant. Thankfully, he was diligent and introduced me to a professional who would do all the searching and negotiation for me. It was a big act of trust for me at the time to send this "pro" $500 electronically to find my car, but a few days later he told me he had negotiated a steal for a brand-new Mazda Miata convertible. I ended up putting $3k down for the car – *under budget*. Of course, I now had a car payment, but I'd never have to worry about serious general repair costs.

By the end of the week, I was on my way up to San Francisco to visit a client in my brand-new convertible. It was more than I ever could've dreamed. It was my first time ever experiencing a brand-new car as my own. I believe this manifestation seemed to exceed my expectation because I wasn't so attached to the make, model, or specifics of the car... I was far more focused on how I would *feel in it*. The universe operates on energies, so it turns out a used car was not an energetic match for the intensely liberating vibes I was putting out... but a brand-new convertible was! I named the car *Amrita*, which translates from Sanskrit as *Nectar of the Gods*. In tantric lineages, *Amrita* is also known as the fluid which dispels from the aroused yoni (aka, squirting). As my car was created by sex magic, it felt right to make *Amrita* the namesake. Not only did this car bring me the joy and freedom I craved in this chapter, but she also empowered me with an ability to expand my reach and impact in my purpose-driven business.

What happens if it doesn't work?

In short, there's something better in store for you. In fact, when I'm manifesting, I end my practice by acknowledging the genius of the universe by saying, *"All this or better."* There have been many things I've "asked for" which I never "received" because an even better opportunity was available for me. We can see this outcome in the story of how I manifested my car above. I was willing to settle for a used convertible, so that's what I asked the universe for, when in reality I had the opportunity to step into a more expansive level of abundance in a brand-new vehicle.

If something isn't working with your manifestations, get curious about why that may be. Are you being too rigidly focused on the outcome, instead of curious about the infinite ways the universe can meet your deepest desire? Desires that are focused more on a physical outcome, such as calling in money, a partner, or a physical thing, are representative of a quality you desire to feel. For example, calling in a partner may represent the desire to feel love, commitment, and connection. What if your most aligned path to these qualities is actually self-love or connection through community or healing your relationship to your parents? That's not to say that you will never receive the soulmate you desire, but maybe there's an opportunity to meet that love from a more whole and expansive place by going through a season of self-love first.

A possible shortcut to manifesting your desires is to instead focus on what is blocking you. This means at the peak of orgasm, instead of zeroing in on the thing you want, say something along the lines of, *"Dear Universe, please show me why I'm always broke… or attracted to unavailable men… or why no one will hire me."* And be ready for the universe to deliver this awareness to you, most likely by triggering you. In chapter 7, I shared a story about this kind of transformative manifestation experience. I asked the universe what was getting in the way of me living my most abundant life and the next day I went on a first date that brought up a lot of limiting beliefs I had about money.

The beauty of this is *we know it's coming*. When we ask the universe to make us aware of our blind spots, we meet our lives with curiosity, almost as if we're on a scavenger hunt. It all becomes a glorious game. We are *expecting* to be triggered because we know that's where our honey pot is. What we desire is there for us, but often our own ego, limiting beliefs, or conditionings are getting in the way. We can't see it because it's too close to home. We're stuck in patterns of familiarity. This is the shortcut.

STEP 7: CELEBRATE YOUR SEX MAGIC SUCCESS.

I am *so* guilty of getting what I want and then immediately focusing on the *next best thing*. It is a divinely feminine quality to always be in desire of *more* and *better*. This quality has gotten me very far in life AND it can be limiting. When we *rush on to the next* we aren't allowing ourselves to fully receive the fruits of our labor. It's like mindlessly wolfing down the cake you spent all day baking, without acknowledging the help of cosmic chemistry and many farmers, producers, and other hands who cultivated and brought the ingredients into your kitchen. It honestly feels disrespectful when you think of it that way, does it not? Consider choosing a method of celebration at the same time that you set your intention. For example, *When I sign my first client I will buy myself a new, professional wardrobe.* How will you celebrate and fully receive the invocation of your desires? I believe it to be truly magical that we *get used to* new levels of abundance, that the fireworks of new love become a familiar blanket, that we outgrow what was once our dream home, that, generally, as our standards rise, we have a new energetic minimum for quality of opportunities, connections, and material possessions in our lives. It keeps us evolving and expanding, but, as we learned from step five, gratitude is the attitude of abundance.

When you want what you want, but you don't know how to get it, let go and let God, and by God I mean the life force that brought you into the world. By becoming an ally to your sexuality, not only are you tapping into a fountain of untapped potential, but you're also reframing your relationship to eroticism. You are literally pushing your edges and creating evidence of a new way of interacting with your sexuality. You become empowered by the same energy that used to be shrouded in fear, limiting beliefs, and shame. You go Glen Coco (I had to bring it back to *Mean Girls* – this is a multi-dimensional healing moment).

HOMEPLAY
Sacred Sex Ed integration activities and expansive opportunities to transform the way you make love to life.

SEX MAGIC RITUAL
Supplies: self-pleasure tools, pen, paper, and imagination

Go through the seven stages of sex magic illustrated in this chapter:

1. Set an intention. Allow yourself to want what you want. You'll be harnessing very powerful life force energy in this ritual. Where would you like to direct it?

2. Awaken your Eros. Seduce yourself or each other with full presence and pleasure. Set the mood for this practice. Take your time.

3. Merge intention with life force at climax. Visualize, with gratitude, receiving what you desire. Declare it out loud.

4. Integrate and make space. Let go of anything that isn't serving your intention. If you don't let go of limiting patterns and beliefs, you'll be sending mixed signals and you'll receive mixed results. Consider journaling at this stage.

5. Be grateful for all that you already have. Take a moment to consider the Earth has already so generously provided all your basic needs and so many desires without you ever really needing to make the *ask*.

6. Take action. Consider who you need to become to embody the manifestation you desire. Decide three action items to get the ball rolling.

7. Celebrate your sex magic success. Choose a method of celebration for when your manifestation comes to fruition.

CHAPTER 13:

PUSHING EDGES & UPHOLDING BOUNDARIES

The first few times my husband and I had sex, it truly felt like we were making love. It was powerful, sensual, and energetic. He was my King. My God. I felt like I was an altar that he prayed before. It was exactly what I wanted and expected from sexual intimacy with my life partner. And then one day, he randomly started calling me a *whore* while he fucked me and it didn't stop. Before long *it felt like* most of our sexual interactions were about degrading me. It triggered the shit out of me. I wasn't a hard *no* to being called a whore, but the way it was done felt *yucky*. I needed to be called a Queen just as much, if not more than I was called a whore, at the very least. So, I brought my feelings to his attention, and then HE was triggered. "I feel like you're shaming my sexuality," he countered. "I think you're projecting your sexual trauma onto my desires."

Overall our sex was great, but we went back to this argument every couple of months. We both wanted more. We both felt unsafe to share what we really, really wanted. We both felt like our boundaries were being violated, when in reality, *we were both being invited to push our edges*. In fact, I knew that it could actually be a *turn on* for my partner to call me a whore. But I needed to feel cherished and respected on a foundational level and I didn't always feel that way. Not because he didn't love and cherish me, but because of my perspective of what that would look like. Andrew loved worshiping me, but he felt resentful that I didn't seem to go all in on his desires, too. And at the root of it all, Andrew and I both have trust issues and can be control freaks – having control brings us the illusion of safety. Of course, our partners are such incredible mirrors for our growth and expansion. It was incredibly edgy for both of us to completely surrender to the other in this activated space, even though we deeply loved each other and had already committed our lives to one another. We were offering each other *breakthroughs* on a silver platter, but we couldn't quite get there from our *breakdowns*. We were hiding behind our own egos as well as our "boundaries".

As we learned from chapters 8 and 9, we know boundaries can be liberating and create safety. I'm a firm believer in having strong boundaries. When lovers tell me their *noes,* I'm much more trusting and convinced of their *yeses*. In fact, when I have a safer sex convo and someone says they have no boundaries, I feel skeptical and often reconsider connecting with them at all. I often invite them to name at least one boundary, even if it sounds ridiculous, such as *no punching me in the face* or *do not poop on me*.

Boundaries are like a fence – a structure creating space for unabashed expression and flow. Imagine if you were led to the edge of a cliff, blindfolded, and then asked to dance. I bet your dancing would be very calculated and cautious, tiptoeing around so you didn't dance right off that cliff. You would be very in your head and not able to let your body move you. Now, imagine a large and sturdy fence was built five feet from the edge of the cliff – a boundary. Once again, you are blindfolded and asked to dance wildly. I bet, in this case, you could actually move freely with authenticity. When we set boundaries, we are erecting an energetic fence that empowers us to move with freedom. When used intentionally, boundaries create space for greater spontaneity and expansion.

But sometimes, we hide behind our boundaries. We hide behind our limitations. We play small and stay in our lane. Sometimes we use boundaries as a way to stay in our victimhood or to avoid the fun-comfortable sensations of courage, risk, and growth. *What would it look like to be empowered in our boundaries, while also creating space for expansion?* That would be pushing your edges.

Let's go back to our fence analogy: The fence, which is five feet from the cliff, represents your boundary. We don't want to cross that, but what if we could snap our fingers and *push* the fence back one foot? Woooo – more space to play! *This is beautiful. Let me feel it. Oh, wow. I love this. I'm so happy that I pushed that edge, because it created all of this spaciousness.* And we feel safe because there's still four feet between the cliff and the fence. I could even handle moving the fence back another foot, but that would probably be enough for me. A fence three feet from the edge of the cliff is my *hard boundary*. This is what *pushing your edges* looks like – finding your boundary and seeing if there's an invitation to create more space there.

Let's say we built the fence at three feet from the cliff's drop-off from the get-go. Maybe we try to push that edge another foot. *AH – nope. Hard boundary – nice try!* Some boundaries are hard, meaning there is no edge to push. *That's okay!* Pushing edges means getting curious about your boundaries, considering why they're there, and creating space (if it's available!) to expand outside of our comfort zone.

WHEN TO LEAN IN

I have an unpopular opinion. Many spiritual and sex-positive communities encourage us to take on the belief *"If it's not a fuck-yes, it's a fuck-no."*

I'm a fuck-no to this mentality. On the surface, I get it. I do agree we should *really* feel into our bodies before making decisions and honor what comes up. But I also find this adage *super* limiting. I'm generally not a big fan of extreme black and white. It's just not very tantric. If I'm not a fuck-yes to something, I get real clear on where the resistance is coming from. Is the opportunity very clearly causing me to sacrifice my needs, boundaries, or values? If so, then maybe it is a fuck-no, or at least I get to be curious about what I'm sacrificing for.

On the other hand, very often the resistance comes up because the opportunity is *just* outside our comfort zone. It feels edgy. Our ego and the part of us that wants to survive wants to feel safe, and our comfort zone is safe. But conversely there's a lot of juicy life, lessons, and liberation just outside the comfort zone. When you're not a fuck-yes, maybe it's your ego trying to keep you small. Maybe it's your past trauma getting in your way. Perhaps it's societal conditioning that makes it feel safer if you follow the pack? It's worth getting curious about.

The *"If it's not a fuck-yes, it's a fuck-no"* perspective can be really disempowering, especially to people who are able to consent to a sexual act without jumping for joy about it. Sex workers and asexual individuals may appear to be quite different on the surface, but they both may experience this sensation more regularly. Both may consent to sex without feeling completely turned on by the idea, but still genuinely want to give it a go or are at least open to exploring sexually, albeit for likely different reasons or motivations. We ALL do things from time to time that we're not a *full fuck-yes about* for one reason or another. Let your decision to lean into other parts of your life give you permission to consider the bigger picture sexually as well.

When Andrew and I both felt our boundaries were being crossed and our desires were not being met, we had the fun-comfortable opportunity to get curious about whether we could push our edges. After months of circling this argument, we were walking on the beach during a vacation. The night before we had both been really triggered by the whore-ish debacle. I suggested we each take turns *having it all the way our way*, meaning I had one chance to be completely treated like a Queen, worshiped head to toe with lots of sensual and energetic touch. Andrew was to completely facilitate this for me, surrendering to my desire. And then a few days later, I would become his whore... I would come into the bedroom already warmed up and ready to be ravished. He would have his way with me and I would surrender to *his* desire. It was edgy for both of us, and Andrew was especially skeptical. Being the sweetheart he is, he didn't foundationally want to have sex with me in a way that wasn't a full yes for me. And I wasn't totally sure I would be, but I knew it was an edge I was willing to push. I literally dropped to my knees on the beach and begged him to let me be his whore. That night, we penciled in two "intimacy nights" on our calendar, one labeled *Tantra Queen Night* and the other *Whore Date Night*.

Penciling in those two dates created safety for both of us. We didn't commit to this structure for the rest of our lives; we committed to two days as a trial. When pushing edges, it helps to create a structure of framework so you feel you can backtrack or redirect if needed.

Another way I created safety was by getting more clarity. I checked in with myself to consider why I was so resistant to being called a whore. Logically, I had no problem with it. The word itself etymologically means Holy Woman. The hora in Hebrew is a sacred dance of harlots, brides of God. "Prostitute" has roots originating from "prostrating" (lying) at the altar. So a prostitute may be defined as one who lies at the altar. Whether she lies there to pray or to have sex...? *Maybe they're the same thing?*

Over thousands of years, these words and the women behind them have been demonized and cast out. But my mission has been to reclaim them – to help people see the integration of their spirituality and sexuality. So when Andrew called me a whore, you'd think I'd own it on principle. But in my mind, I had created a story that he was intending to degrade me, like we so often see in porn and all over the world in brothels. I equated it with him using me or treating me like an animal. Realizing I had no real evidence of this *story* being true, I asked Andrew how he would define a whore.

He said something along the lines of "being so hungry for my cock, you will do anything to have it." Well, that's a definition I could get behind, because *it was true for me*! I love this man and I love his cock and on more than one occasion, I've had to seduce him to get what I want: his cock. He also specified, "You're MY whore. No one else's. I don't want you being whore-ish for anyone else." Ahhh, so basically, Andrew just wanted me to be really excited to have primal, messy sex with him. Having this context in my brain made it much easier to surrender fully into his desire, because I wasn't stuck in my head considering if I was compromising my values and truth.

Sometimes it feels like we are speaking a different language, which is why asking our partner to define the words they use can be incredibly eye-opening and diplomatic. When it comes to pushing your edges, get curious about what you need to feel safe and empowered. For me that looked like having a trial timeline and getting more clarity on the intention and motivation of all parties.

Later that week, we had very sweet, connective, and stereotypically tantric sex. It was exactly what I wanted, and Andrew confessed it was what we needed in that moment to come back to love, laying an even more solid foundation for our union. A few days later, I slipped into a slutty little outfit and became his whore. It was fun and I loved bringing my man the raunchy pleasure he desired. He felt totally accepted and met. Since then, we've been able to organically flow between our desires based on what we feel will be the most connective and expansive for our relationship.

Pushing your edges can transcend your sex life and intimacy patterns – it can become *a part of your lifestyle*, which leads to maximum growth and collapsed timelines. If I hadn't pushed my edges, I would have robbed myself of the opportunity to break through my limiting beliefs. I would have robbed myself of the sacred play it became to take on the role of *whore*. I would have robbed our relationship of the next layer of depth available for us.

CALCULATED RISK AND REWARD

I've made a spiritual practice of *doing the thing I'm most afraid of.* Fear is a survival mechanism, but **the things we do to survive are not always the same things that will empower us to thrive.** Every time I've committed to doing something scary, it has led to the most transformative periods of my life. I literally wouldn't be writing this book or working *on purpose* if it weren't for consistently pushing my edges and doing the thing I was most afraid of.

What feels like a lifetime ago, in my early twenties, I was a digital nomad, meaning I worked online and traveled the world. I primarily lived in countries with a relatively low cost of living, like Romania, Morocco, South Africa, and Mexico. My base expenses were usually less than $1k a month. I did this for three years and it became quite comfortable for me. Despite all the exciting adventure, I began to feel stagnant. I intuitively knew moving back to the States and finding community was my next growth edge. I felt called to move to LA, but that terrified me. *It's so expensive. I'm not cool enough to live in LA. I'm going to have to get a 9-5 job to make that work. You can only make it in LA if you come from a wealthy family.* But I just knew I had to go.

I made a plan in my mind that created a sense of structure and safety to push this edge. First, I decided I would give it three months. If in three months, I was struggling to fit in and pay my bills, I would go back to being a digital nomad. Second, I reached out to some local LA businesses and brands, offering my creative services to do freelance work. This way I had something tying me to the place and supporting me financially. And then *I did it!* I got a cheap, small sublet in Hollywood. At $1200/month, it was more than I had ever spent on rent. I was previously paying $300/month for my studio in Eastern Europe. My expenses basically quadrupled and it was very edgy.

After three months in LA, I was treading water. I wasn't drowning. I was making it work. I decided to give it a year. And suddenly, those three months turned into three of the most impactful years of my life. It was in those three years that I went all in on Tantra as a lifestyle and as my soul's work. I wouldn't have done so without the incredible spiritual community in LA. When I launched my business, I was supported by what seemed to be unlimited demands for my gifts. I met my mentor in California. I worked through my scarcity mindset and low self-worth. I made lifelong friends and had several incredible relationships, which prepared me for lifetime partnership. *If I hadn't done the thing that scared me most, I would have robbed myself of all these opportunities.*

Committing to a Tantra lifestyle is not all sunshine and rainbows – it's equally an invitation into the darkest night of your soul. It's a courageous path of radical honesty, vulnerability, and divine risk. As we embrace our fears and pain, we meet the joy of truly living. By pushing our edges, we are energetically telling the universe, "*I am willing to take the risk of pain in the name of divine love.*"

HOMEPLAY
Sacred Sex Ed integration activities and expansive opportunities to transform the way you make love to life.

EXPLORING THE EDGE
Supplies: pen and paper

1. Journal three things that used to intimidate you, but you now enjoy or feel neutral towards:

_____
_____
_____

2. Journal three things out of your comfort zone you'd like to know more about:

_____
_____
_____

3. Journal three things you've tried that are simply not for you:

_____
_____
_____

CHAPTER 14:
SACRED SURRENDER

Do not be fooled, sacred sexuality and Tantra are not exclusively defined by super slow sex and unwavering eye contact. While Tantra does invite initiates to slow down for the purpose of dropping into the body, evoking presence and intention, that doesn't mean things can't ramp up into primal, messy, and dark play. In fact, consciously and intentionally using BDSM and kink as tools to explore the depths of humanity can be liberating and healing. In my opinion, it is just as spiritual to deep-throat cock as it is to meditate – in fact, they're kind of the same thing, when done intentionally.

Recall from chapter 5 that the Sanskrit word for cock is *lingam*, which is associated with the God Shiva and penetrating consciousness. In meditation, are we not inviting in God? Are we not observing our consciousness? So, literally sucking cock can be a meditative practice in physically embodying our devotion to God. In this way, deep-throating isn't just for those on the receiving end. While penis owners are nearly certain to enjoy the devotional offering of this penetrative act, the honor of holding his vulnerability at the portal of your throat chakra (energetic center) has the capacity to induce mind-altering states and open portals of authentic expression. To receive all this penetrative potential in the same mouth that voices your desires and dreams should not be taken as a coincidence. There's opportunity here. While a blowjob requires more active worship, deep-throating calls for a *sacred surrender.* Anything less creates tension in the body and mind, and a less than expansive experience. It gets to be messy, invoking a primal, intuitive, and meditative state for both parties.

Throat contractions and purge while deep-throating are totally normal here – no wonder they are common in the throat chakra (energetic center) with a shadow of swallowing our truths. We use massage, acupressure, and bodywork to de-armor and soften tension in other parts of our body. Deep-throating can create a similar sensation and release in the throat. My advice: Wait until BOTH parties are already aroused and start slow. Create a hand signal to communicate when you need to come up for air.

This quality of *surrender* is a common theme amongst many BDSM and kink practices. As a recovering control freak with very real trust issues, surrender is an act I've struggled with yet learned to love. I used to define surrender exclusively as giving my power away – waving the white flag in defeat. I also disliked the religious context of *surrendering to God*. I didn't appeal to the idea of giving my power away to some omnipotent white man who lived in the sky. That didn't feel good for me, especially when I didn't wholeheartedly agree with the contradictory and judgy messaging that *Jesus loves everyone*, but if you sin *you will go to hell*. I have done a complete 180 on this and now invite God to take over pretty much every day of my life. And a big piece of that had to do with exploring the concept of surrender through BDSM. Wild.

RECEIVING AND RESISTANCE

Objectively, my clients that struggle the most with Tantra are those that struggle the most with surrender. One foundation of my one-on-one in-person sessions is to allow the initiate to fully receive. So often in intimate settings, our brain is working out how to dance within a realm of giving and receiving. It is so rare that we are invited to just relax without the pressure (self-imposed or otherwise) to reciprocate for our partner, lover, or even friend. Even more rare, when given this opportunity to receive without the expectation of reciprocation, it can feel impossible to sit back, relax, and enjoy it without our brains running 90 miles per minute. When we are fully in receive-mode, we can be truly present with our bodies to witness the magic of life force energy moving through it.

In my work, you learn to recognize these energies within your body and, more importantly, how to harness them for maximum pleasure and ecstatic benefits. During one-on-one Tantra ceremonies and during group events or retreats, I spend a long time easing initiates into a relaxed and receptive space by using tools of movement and meditation. But there are always those who are resistant; those who can't keep their eyes closed during the meditation, who try to veer the session in another direction, or who project their sexual energy onto me or other participants rather than allowing themselves to fully feel in their own bodies. They are usually very successful men who have come to their level of success by control; they have rightly been rewarded for their discipline and ability to lead. Other times they are women who have been burned very badly in the past and are deeply afraid of letting themselves be vulnerable ever again. Either way, this is not bad; in fact, it is very good in many contexts. But they come to me to *let go*.

When I notice a client or participant is especially resistant to being in a receptive space, I put a blindfold on them. If they're still resistant, I'll suggest one of two things for an upcoming session: a water ritual or shibari. The water ritual involves getting into a bath, which mimics the womb. The womb is the ultimate surrender and it is the first act of surrender our soul makes when coming into this world – to be in the void, the unknown, the darkness. This alone is often enough to relax and soften individuals into fully receiving. Other times, shibari is very effective.

A few years into my practice, I started both giving and receiving shibari, a form of rope bondage originating in Japan. Shibari was originally used as a sort of torture and humiliation device for prisoners, but it has since been adapted by the BDSM community to make art of dominant/submissive dynamics. To be tied up in a way that limits or completely hinders mobility requires a very solid foundation of trust in the dominant, and it can become an incredibly profound meditative practice for the submissive. The first time I was suspended as a shibari sub, meaning I was bound and then lifted off the floor to hang from a beam on the ceiling, I felt like I was cradled in the womb. It was not sexual at all, as shibari is not inherently an erotic practice (similar to Tantra, it has been increasingly sexualized by practitioners and enthusiasts). It had a transcendental quality that initiated ancestral healing. The experience was beyond words, as I find many shamanic practices to be. In these lineages, it is believed the deeper we explore ourselves, the greater our awareness of the entirety of the universe – *as above, so below*. We are a microcosm of the macrocosm.

It was this experience that inspired me to bring shibari into my Tantra sessions. While I am no pro and certainly will not be suspending initiates into the air any time soon, even very simple ties and wrappings with the rope can invite a profound level of surrender. I knew just who to start with...

I had been working with Robert* on and off for a few years since the early days of my practice. He was also a dedicated listener of my podcast – he once showed me his Spotify account where *Talk Tantra to Me* sat right next to *Joe Rogan* on his "most listened to" section. He was in his thirties, very successful, but he struggled with his romantic relationships. He credited me for changing his life and expanding his perspective of possibility in the world. He was one of my favorite clients, but we could only ever go *so far*. He had a wall up. I could never really get him to fully surrender and receive. So, I suggested we try the ropes. He was very excited about the prospect but didn't really know what he was getting himself into.

I slipped a blindfold over his eyes and put on some tribal trance music. I began tying, using my weight and muscle to hold him up and move him around the mattress on the floor. It was clunky at first as he tried to anticipate my movements and make it "easier" on me by moving himself, but every time he did this, I'd restrain that part of him or move him in the opposite direction. Eventually, he began to soften. I moved slowly and sensually. I felt like I was channeling God, as I lulled him into complete submission. At one point, he was nearly fully restrained (or at least I made it feel that way – in reality he could have easily broken down all of my amateur ties). From this place, we rested; I held him. He felt my breath on his skin. He let out a big sigh. That was it. I slowly began moving again. He was a rag doll of submission. Eventually I unraveled him and slowly took off the blindfold. "I get it now," he said.

When we consciously choose to be blindfolded, tied up, ordered around by our lover, tantrika, dom/domme, or otherwise, *we are making a sacred choice* – a sacred surrender. We are inviting in pure presence; when we give up control, we are able to be with what is. We are literally out of our minds and in our bodies. We are invited to let go and receive with the intention of vulnerability. A sacred surrender can be a catalyst to expansive states of being, soul evolution, and profound freedom. Surrender can be synonymous with freedom, in that it opens portals to new worlds. We actively *surrender* each day – by necessity and innate desire, *we go to sleep*. When we go to sleep, on a very basic level, we are surrendering our sight, but we are also surrendering our connection to time and the constructs of this reality.

Consider all the places your dreams have taken you when you've surrendered to sleep. Meditation can create a similar outcome. Anyone who has given meditation a true, honest try can attest to the inward shift that occurs when we close our eyes, surrendering our sight to focus our attention and energy.

Orgasm is a moment of a surrender. It requires letting the body be taken over with pleasure and ecstatic waves. When one door closes – *when we surrender a part of ourselves* – another door opens. When we let go of control and attachment to an outcome, we invite ourselves into space for full-body pleasure. Any integral professional dominant or dominatrix will tell you that they are not holding all the power in a scene with a submissive. The submissive is in just as much control, if not more. The sub actively *gives* the power and can take it back at any time. It is this choice – this agreement – that illustrates the power of the submissive. The dom/domme is merely *holding* the power of the submissive.

But why would we want someone else to hold our power?

So we can be free to explore ourselves. Without the need to make decisions or facilitate an experience or be at all in our heads, we can be fully embodied. We get to explore the role of *being* while we are completely held by someone who holds the *responsibility* for us. This sacred surrender can lead to a sort of euphoria called *subspace*.

Eva Krockow, lecturer at the University of Leicester, estimates we make more than 35,000 decisions each day. What happens when we surrender the power of decision-making? Many have experienced a rush of serotonin that leaves them speechless, giddy, or impeccably relaxed. Known as *subspace*, this quality of being has been associated with both heaven and heroin. I would argue both addicts and Bible Belters relate to the come-to-Jesus invitation offered by sacred surrender.

When we choose sacred surrender, we are really choosing ourselves. We are surrendering to the divine within us, which so conveniently connects us all. I now see myself as a Divine Being (i.e. God/Goddess), and *that* is who I'm really surrendering to. When I *choose* to surrender (whether it be to God, pain, pleasure, the circumstances of my life, or to a trusted dom/domme), I consider myself to be surrendering to my highest self. I see it as an opportunity to explore my greatest potential to make the most impact in this lifetime. *Yum* – that's the kind of surrender that gets my pussy wet.

By the same token, the more willing we are to receive our pain and other dense emotions, the greater our capacity to experience love and pleasure. When we explore the pleasure of primal sexuality (sometimes explored through S&M), including biting, scratching, and spanking, we have the capacity to open portals to expanded consciousness and receivership. Spanking, for example, becomes a spiritual practice. In addition to the yummy pain portal spanking unveils, hitting the booty can awaken the kundalini energy at our base. Kundalini is synonymous with erotic energy. Spanking can be a great tool in sending the kundalini right up your spine, opening your capacity for full-body ecstasy and pleasure. Prepare your paddles and flogs, my loves… your kundalini awakening awaits.

PERMISSION TO PLAY

Roleplay also has a surrendered quality as we zero in on one archetype within us and bring it into expression with a beloved. In the previous chapter on pushing edges, I shared how taking on the role of *whore* allowed me and my partner to widen our range of sexual expression. I was invited to explore my limiting beliefs and assumptions of sacred sluttery in my partnership. This resulted in more connection and satisfaction for both of us in and out of the bedroom.

Many roleplay fantasies are built on the foundation of a predator and prey relationship. There is an innate naturalness in this dynamic, as we are all primal animals deep down. Having a safe space to fully surrender into these roles can be incredibly empowering and holistic. In fact, there is a cost to leaving these desires in the shadow. The awareness of our fullness, including our shadowy desires and fears, holds power. And as we learned from previous chapters, we often project these fears and desires onto our lives and relationships if left unchecked.

I once worked with a man in my Sacred Intimacy virtual mentorship. He was the quintessential *good guy* – so much so that he often became a self-sacrificing martyr. This wasn't good for him or for anyone else. But, because he is human, like everyone else, he also had fantasies and dark desires. He once confessed one of his old girlfriends was coming over to hang out with him and his new girlfriend. It was meant to be totally platonic, but he found himself plotting how to get them both in bed. *Scandalous!*

This thought was not bad or wrong, but before he fully owned this desire, he was unconsciously projecting his shadow desire into his relationship to manipulate an outcome.

When we unpacked this, he had permission to privately revel in his fantasy and then decide if it was something he actually wanted to consider and request from these two women. He also became aware of other places in his life where he wasn't owning his desires and he got to have some of his racier fantasies fulfilled in safe, consensual containers.

For further resources on owning our dark desires and meeting them in an integral place, consider reading *The Erotic Mind* by Dr. Jack Morin and *Existential Kink* by Carolyn Elliott, PhD.

When we have the audacity to own our edgiest, kinkiest, and most primal desires, not only are we creating the potential for them to be fulfilled, but we also become evidence of vulnerability and authenticity. We become inspiration for others to own their own desires. At many Tantra play parties or temple nights, I like to introduce a game called Mildest and Wildest. Participants split up into small groups and go around in a circle, first sharing the *mildest* thing that could happen that night that would leave them feeling satisfied with their experience of the event. A *mildest* desire could be eye-gazing, having really good conversation, getting a foot rub, kissing a stranger, vanilla sex, etc. Then, participants share their *wildest* desire for the evening. A *wildest* desire is within their boundaries but may be pushing an edge. Examples may include group sex, trying a new sex toy, interacting sexually with the same gender for the first time, double penetration, etc.

After sharing in small groups, we often open the floor for popcorn sharing, inviting several individuals to share their *mildest* and/or *wildest* in front of the whole room. One time, a man bravely stood up and shared his wildest desire was to receive a golden shower (to be urinated on) by a woman. Once we opened the container for free play, not one... not two... not three... but *four women* said they were willing to satisfy his desire. That man will go down in the history books as a legend of play parties and a champion for owning one's desire.

HOMEPLAY
Sacred Sex Ed integration activities and expansive opportunities to transform the way you make love to life.

GOD IS MY DOM
Supplies: self-pleasure tool and imagination

I don't know about you, but I feel closest to God on the brink of orgasm, so what better time to converse with the divine than during a masturbation session? This pleasure practice is similar to a sex magic ritual, in that you are encouraged to connect to the infinite potential of the universe, yet the intention is focused on inviting God (or your highest self) to work through you.

1. Set an intention. Lean into the energy of the universe supporting you. Ask for clarity.

2. Awaken your Eros. Seduce yourself with full presence and pleasure. The more you're able to build this energy with edging or waves of arousal, the stronger your life force becomes.
Bonus Tip: I love to self-restrict parts of my body with shibari ropes before this type of ritual to amplify the energy of surrender. You can buy your own rope and find tutorials online (see the resources section). Make sure you have scissors nearby. Safety first!

3. Merge intention with Eros at climax. At climax, especially as you orgasm and immediately after, ask the universe (or your higher self or God) what matters most? Rather than focusing on an outcome you desire, like you would in sex magic, allow yourself to become receptive. Surrender to something higher moving through you.

4. Listen. Objectively observe any feelings, visualizations, sensations, thoughts, etc. that may come through in this moment. Let go of attachment – hold space for whatever is available. Expecting guidance to come through in an obvious or familiar way may distract you from other possibilities. In the following days, be open to guidance/signs from spirit.

HOMEPLAY
Sacred Sex Ed integration activities and expansive opportunities to transform the way you make love to life.

FROM SHAME TO SHADOW WORK
Supplies: pen, paper, and your imagination!

1. Journal about your "dirtiest" fantasy or fetish – the one that you feel guilty and ashamed about. The one that makes you clear your search history after getting off. The one that gives you a pit in your stomach, makes your heart thump, and your loins moisten.

2. Find a quiet and secluded space to meditate on this imagery as an objective observer.

3. Do a body scan to see where the judgment is living in your body. Breathe into it and let it go.

4. Give yourself permission to fully enjoy this kink, acknowledging you are in a safe container to do so.

5. Ask yourself where this desire might have come from. Maybe the adrenaline rush excites you... maybe the idea of being out of control... maybe the sense of full surrender to receive... Think about it!

6. If you're still feeling intrigued by the kink after your meditation, consider one thing you can do to bring it into reality. To go deeper in a safe container – maybe it's a trip to the sex shop... or a nudist colony... a retreat. Maybe it's sharing your desire with your partner... a sex therapist... or sacred intimate. How can you give yourself permission to love your darkness?

CHAPTER 15:

BECOMING A PLEASURE PRIESTESS

What does it mean to be a pleasure priest or priestess? Who is the holy whore? The sacred prostitute? And is it *for you*? To be a pleasure priest or priestess is to be dedicated to mastering the energy that made you – your life force energy. This path is available to anyone and everyone. You can be a pleasure priest/ess just for yourself, for your lover, or for the whole world. It can be an energy you call on now and again, a lifestyle you commit to, or an expression of your grander purpose in a professional setting. The pleasure priest/ess is an archetype that can exist within all of us should we choose to call her forth by embodying the principles in this text, or by embodying the principles that create expansion and liberation *for you*.

As I've shared in previous chapters, my entry point to shamanic sexuality and Tantra was very much focused on myself – on my healing. I was on a journey to be turned on by life itself. But the deeper I went inward, the more I desired to expand outward, to share the possibilities with the world. There were a few turning points in which I went from following the Tantra path to leading others on the path. In that season of life, I was a freelance creative, artist, and storyteller. One of my clients was a non-profit based in South Asia. Their mission, to free children from sex trafficking, deeply touched me. I was honored when they invited me to come to India to help them film a documentary, with the intention to raise awareness and garner funds.

That week in Mumbai, we met with survivors, law enforcement, and social workers. We toured the red-light district, as well as the slums. I even rode along on a legitimate raid, where several young girls were freed and the perpetrators were arrested. My role was to facilitate the interviews, creating a storyline and arc for the documentary. Alongside a translator, I had the opportunity to get incredibly intimate with the survivors, the organization, and cause. I so appreciate the work they are doing – freeing the innocent and arresting the bad guys. And yet, I noticed something missing – we weren't getting to the root cause... we weren't addressing *the demand*... we weren't looking at **why** these perpetrators felt the only way they'd get their sexual desire met was by raping a child.

At this point in my life, I was deeply integrated in a Tantra lifestyle, but I wasn't practicing it professionally. I would offer suggestions and readings to friends and people who organically fell into my path. It didn't feel like my place to teach Tantra, nor did I feel qualified. But as I interviewed these young women and the individuals who worked tirelessly to free them, I couldn't help but consider how sacred sex could completely disrupt the demand for sexual violence.

It was in this realization that it dawned on me how disconnected we are as a collective from the sacredness of sexuality and how damaging societal conditioning can be. The integration of sacred sex and Tantra directly addresses and has the power to eliminate atrocities such as sexual violence. Ironically, I've heard from many modern Indians who follow my podcast and a few guests (including Henika Patel, founder of the School of Sensual Arts, and Oorja Makkad, founder of Revive.Style) that many citizens of India fear Tantra and see it as a form of black magic, despite the fact that Tantra originates in this part of the world. Then and there I realized it was my *duty* to do this work. The world needs it.

A lot of imposter syndrome came up, being just one woman, but I trusted my internal compass and began sharing more and more of the teachings that helped me. All those years ago, I never imagined my work would actually touch the populations that worked on that documentary. But within months of launching the *Talk Tantra to Me* podcast, I had listeners from India reaching out with praise and excitement – two (so far!) even came on the podcast and shared with their local audience in India!

Since embarking on this path, I have worked with thousands of people. I've hosted hundreds of Tantra ceremonies and rituals for couples and individuals, I've coached one-on-one and in group containers, I've led sold out retreats, facilitated play parties, and taught at Tantra festivals. I get daily messages of gratitude for *Talk Tantra to Me,* my free podcast – my most accessible offering. I'm dedicated to this work because of the transformation I see possible for individuals and for the world. I've helped repair marriages and families. I've been a safe space for individuals to discover what they really want in the bedroom *and in life*! I've coached others in stepping into their purpose – helping them create their own businesses and offerings to make an impact in the world.

It's time more men and women allow themselves to get intimate with the archetype of the pleasure priestess, purely by being evidence of what is possible for yourself and for those in your life. Our society glorifies some divine feminine archetypes, such as the nurturing mother, the fruitful maiden, the supple virgin, but conveniently demonizes the whore, the prostitute, and the witch. Evidence of ancient and more matriarchal and nature-led societies honored the wholeness of the feminine. They intimately understood the sacred relationship between the physical world and the spiritual world. They were in deep reverence of the energy that links these two worlds: life force, or sexual energy. They approached sexuality as a sacred act and worshiped goddesses of fertility, such as Inanna, Isis, and Ishtar. All over the ancient world, including the cradle of humanity in Mesopotamia, Egypt, and Greece, there were temples in which initiates would meet with the priestesses who served as embodiments of the Holy Goddess. They worshiped these women and, in some cases, had sex with them.

In these ancient times, it was these priestesses who initiated kings. All over the ancient world, including Babylonia, Sumer, and Greece, when warriors returned from battle, they didn't go straight home to their families. First they went to the temples to meet with the Goddess, who brought them back into their bodies. These sacred prostitutes softened their hearts and reminded them of their humanity after the coldness of war. The priestesses would bathe and massage them, tending to their emotional, physical, and spiritual wounds. In some cases, she would expand her own energetic field to alchemize the wounded energy and de-armor his heart. He would return to his family without the PTSD our own troops are known to suffer from.

In these ancient times, newlyweds would travel to the temples to learn the arts of intimacy and divine union. Some say the word *honeymoon* originates from the concept of making a pilgrimage after marriage during the warm months by the light of the full moon to be received by the priests and priestesses. These holy men and women would teach the young couple divine arts of sacred union, or *heiros gamos*. Even today, the full moon in June is known as the Honey Moon, and year after year, June is one of the most popular months to wed. Today, the honeymoon is widely adopted by couples as a holiday after the wedding, in which it is generally expected to have lots of sex! My work with couples is built upon giving couples the tools to tap into the energy of their *honeymoon,* regardless of the season and longevity of their relationship.

Under a new moon in June, I once worked with a couple married over 20 years. We spent three days together in Joshua Tree. The first night we set intentions and I gave them a few devotional practices to honor themselves, each other, and their relationship. They met their bodies as temples to their inner divine. I had them eye gaze and yoni gaze and meet each other with affirmations. We closed the ceremony under a starry sky in a hot tub overlooking the desert. "Every couple should learn this on their honeymoon," the wife said. "I shouldn't have to wait 20 years to have a connection like this with my husband. I haven't looked into his eyes like that or for that long since I was standing at the altar." Words like these make me melt.

REMEMBRANCE AND RECLAMATION

It is our true nature to have deeply connective, healing, and empowering sex. We are born with this capability – we have merely learned to do otherwise. So much of this path involves peeling back these layers to come home to our true essence. I've even come to a place of deep gratitude for the sexual violence, collective trauma, and societal conditioning I've experienced. I have a profound recognition that my sexual assault has allowed me to step into my purpose more authentically. I have healed the trauma around my sexual assault, which means that I can help others do the same and I can guide them in letting go of their shame, their guilt, their trauma, because I did it. So I love that I experienced it. I love that I am a rebel in today's society. I love that every day I get to challenge the status quo, to redefine what it means to be a modern sexually empowered woman. I get to remind people of their power. *How cool is that?*

I used to hold so much judgment of the sexual side of myself. As I stepped into this space professionally, I had even more fear that I'd be considered a sex worker. I worried men would not commit to me because of how generously I overflow into the world; because of how easy it is for me to see the best in others and want to love all of them for it. I worried they'd want to keep all of me and my gifts to themselves. I worried women would ostracize me. Blame me for loving their men too openly. Feel threatened by the fullness of my expression.

It's a delicate balance – not taking the triggered reactions of others personally, while also appreciating the evidence of so much reciprocal love from those in alignment. It is an initiation to release mind drama, in favor of trusting my ability to offer commitment and consistency and also my worthiness of receiving it back. Now I know my sacred slut deserves love. My slut IS love giving itself freely. Because love is limitless, she doesn't want to play small in how she spends it. My expansive Eros makes me more lovable. My perspective of love and sex makes me *more* attractive and lovable. I am a magnet for receiving love that feels *out of this world*, because the evolved love I am a match for is beyond this planet's current capacity. I am where the magic is – and anyone who can't see that isn't ready for my magic anyways. *The same goes for you.*

I have even gone so far as to reclaim the meaning of sex work. Times are changing. Systems are crumbling and sex work can evolve alongside the expansion into higher states of consciousness. To be a sex worker in an evolved paradigm is to be the living embodiment of limitless love. The evolved sex worker has fully integrated their spiritual and sexual self, inspiring others to do the same. They are magnetic beings worthy of unwavering devotion and love. According to this definition, I can proudly say, "I am a sex worker."

Professionally speaking, sexual energy is a cornerstone of my work. The sex work I do is very different from traditional sex work, in that there is no penetrative sex and I'm more focused on empowering people to master their life force energy and heal their trauma, rather than meeting a desire. But I truly believe even simply meeting a desire, fulfilling a fantasy, or offering loving, erotic touch can be super high-vibration, expansive, and healing. When done with integral intentions, even traditional sex work can offer people safety, permission, and connection. In this way, I do not believe there is anything wrong with exchanging money for sex of any kind, in that it is all sacred.

BECOMING THE INITIATION

Being a professional pleasure priestess can manifest in an infinite number of ways. If you feel drawn to this sacred calling, know that **your unique perspective and gifts are not only welcome, but they're needed.** Just like with Tantra, there is no right or wrong way to do it – you get to decide what feels the most juicy and expansive for you to bring to the world! You get to decide how deep you want to go, how naked you want to be, and who you want to go there with. It is my belief that there is no population on this Earth who wouldn't benefit from this work in some way, shape, or form. Consider how you can be the embodiment of the pleasure priestess – do the work by being *you*. For inspiration on the infinite ways of embodying this calling, check out, *Healers on the Edge* by Caffyn Jesse, Cassie Moore, and Mehdi Darvish Yahya and *Reclaiming Eros* by Suzanne Blackburn.

Being the embodiment of sexual liberation, sovereignty, and self-love is a rebellious act. Be prepared to ruffle some feathers and trigger your loved ones and strangers alike. It's a part of the gig. On that topic, I've saved one of my and Andrew's favorite stories to tell for this last chapter. While I'm very rebellious, Andrew came to our relationship more conservative. We are yin and yang perfection. About two months into dating, he invited me to church. I hadn't been to church in nearly 15 years and, honestly, didn't really want to go. But it was important to him, and I noticed my resistance was coming from a place of fear, due to my own upbringing and experience with the Christian church. At this time in my journey, I had already reclaimed my relationship to Jesus and Mary Magdalene (see chapter 4), so it felt like a healthy growth edge to give it a go at the local non-denominational service. That Sunday morning, I got ready naked in front of the mirror, joking with Andrew, "Do you like my outfit for church? God made it for me." We both chuckled about my birthday suit until I revealed to Andrew what I'd actually be wearing.

If I were to go to the *temple,* which is church, I felt called to dress as a *priestess.* So I shimmied into this gorgeous, strappy red dress and wrapped a shawl over my shoulders. I truly felt like Mary Magdalene incarnate. But when I stepped out, Andrew was not impressed. In fact, he was super triggered. He interpreted my choice in clothing as disrespectful to him and to the church. He worried about what people would say about him with this *slutty* girl on his arm. Truth be told, as I was getting dressed I very naively thought my outfit was no big deal. I was just being myself. I was a bit surprised by his reaction. That's the shadow of the inner rebel – being naive to the potential consequences. But I held my truth immaculately and called him forth in the process. Andrew refused to go to church with me *like that.* No matter, "I'll go by myself," I said. I proceeded to order an Uber, leaving him picking his nails behind his computer screen to consider where God landed in all of this.

Off I went to church in my pleasure priestess garb. The ironic thing about all of this is that these church-people claim to love everyone and forgo judgment. So, in truth, my outfit would give these Jesus-Freaks (I say that endearingly and also in kinship) an opportunity to practice what they preach. As I walked into the church, I noticed a few sideways glances in my direction, but nothing more or less than I would expect at any other public establishment. No one shamed me for my clothing, nor did they compliment me for it. I quietly took a place in the back of the packed church. As it turns out, it was their highest attended service yet in the history of the congregation. It was so full that they literally had to close the doors and had a crowd of people watching the sermon on TVs in the lobby. I luckily had snuck in with the last few worshippers and sat in the furthest pew from the altar.

Remember, this was my first time to church in nearly 15 years. It was very emotional for me and brought up a lot of both fond and not-so-fond memories. All in all, I really enjoyed the sermon, but I especially enjoyed the music and singing. Tears streamed down my face as I belted the lyrics posted on the large projector above the stage. I resonated with nearly all of it. The only piece that didn't land was *We are not worthy of God's unconditional love.* Hard pass on that one, but there were plenty other nuggets of gold. During the service, I noticed a few texts from Andrew come through, but I didn't read them, opting to be present with the pastor. At the end of the sermon, I walked out the double doors to find my future husband standing there waiting for me with his watery eyes saying, "Sorry." He pulled me into his arms and we left together.

Holding my truth initiated us both that day. We both had the opportunity to look more clearly at our values, while also releasing what no longer served us. In the end, this conflict brought us closer. And yet, it doesn't always end that way, and you can't expect it to. Not everyone is ready to claim their power and take radical responsibility.

EMBODY THE INITIATION

Do you ever truth bomb super insightful wisdom – the kind that shatters limiting beliefs and has the potential to shift timelines – only for it to be brushed aside? Have you ever invested deep love and care into someone and then had them turn their back on you, opting for society soup? Sometimes our duty is only to plant the seed, not to wait and watch for growth. We're all expanding at our own pace. It may take seasons or even lifetimes for the seed of expansion to take root. One day you'll find someone to dance with in the breeze.

This relationship is the first in which I feel safe to be *all of me*. There were dozens of others that couldn't hold my pleasure priestess in entirety. Dating someone who is so devoted to *a path on the edge* is an extreme initiation not all souls are ready for. I've had friends distance themselves from me and I haven't talked much about my work to my family. To be a pleasure priestess is to be a sacred rebel. The sacred rebel discerns and questions her reality, knowing that just because we've collectively adapted to think and act a particular way, a better and more expansive way can still be found. They lean into love and let go of fear-based ideologies and conditionings. Sacred rebels dare to create a world of liberation and possibility. They don't just dare to dream – *they dare to do it and live it*. That's what it means to be a pleasure priestess – to courageously stand for the highest love for yourself and those around you.

There will be uncomfortable, awkward, and triggering moments, but trust me, it's worth it. It is freedom. The greater our ability to meet the dark, scary parts of ourselves, the greater our capacity to experience profound love and pleasure. So many people come to our retreats very shy, not wanting to be in photos. And it breaks my heart, living in a world that is so repressed we have to hide the most magical parts of ourselves. It also breaks me open to the importance of this work. I feel that with each retreat or event we host, we get a little closer to a more healed, holistic, and loving world. I like to look at this book the same way. I want you to not just taste this freedom, I want you to go all in on the buffet of life. I want you to expand your orgasmic potential, experience greater depths in your relationships, and find like-minded community. I want you to leave the past in the past and have lots of awesome sex.

Which means the wisdom in this book can't simply sit on your bookshelf collecting dust. After you turn this last page, it's time to take what you learned into the world. Recently I went to a book rave birthday party – *yes, my friends are awesome and so creative*. The birthday boy asked us all to bring a book that changed our life, so I brought *Conversations With God* by Neale Donald Walsch. I was 20 years old the first time I picked it up. It was my first "spiritual" book and it was also the first time I witnessed an authority refer to sex as spiritual. My first few years studying sacred intimacy were theoretical, mostly consisting of reading books. I put what I learned into practice in my life and with my partners. It took me far... but only so far.

Books can be portals into higher consciousness. But *it takes integration in community to activate and uplevel*. It's like reading a book about riding a bike compared to actually riding a bike. At this same book rave birthday party, I ran into a participant from one of my recent workshops. I asked him about the book he brought and he said, "This book is great – but what I really need you to know? The tools I learned and **applied** at your last workshop changed my life. Hands-down *the most valuable thing* I've gained in the last five years."

Mind you, this book rave was populated with some of the most impressive entrepreneurs, thought leaders, and master coaches in the country. Everyone there is very much "doing the work." The "tools" he's referring to are introduced at the beginning of every party and retreat we host as a sort of opening circle and workshop (and many are addressed in part 2 of this book). I facilitate Tantra retreats, play parties, and other live experiences because I know the value of connecting in real time to integrate and remember what our bodies innately know. So my invitation to you as we close this journey is to lean into application and integration. Use the tools and the *HomePlay* activities. Share what you learned with your friends and lovers. Get curious, try new things, and have fun! Life gets to be *so much bigger* when you feel safe in the energy that brought you into it.

We need you. The world needs you. We need your gifts, we need your light, and we need as many sexually empowered souls as possible to be evidence of truly holistic liberation.

RESOURCES

CLASSICAL TANTRA

Book
- *Tantra Illuminated: The Philosophy, History, and Practice of a Timeless Tradition*, by Wallis, Christopher D. (Mattamayūra Press, 2013)

Training
- Durga's Tiger School for Tantra Yoga Arts Shamanism, https://www.durgastigertantrayoga.com/

Online Course
- *Turned On By Life Course* by Leola, https://www.talktantratome.com/turned-on

SHAMANIC SEXUALITY & NEO-TANTRA

Books
- *The Sacred Prostitute: Eternal Aspect of the Feminine*, by Qualls-Corbett, Nancy (Inner City Books, 1988)
- *The Magdalen Manuscript: The Alchemies of Horus & The Sex Magic of Isis*, by Magdalene, Mary, et al (Sounds True, Inc, 2006)

- *Urban Tantra: Sacred Sex for the Twenty-First Century*, by Carrellas, Barbara, and Annie Sprinkle (Ten Speed Press, 2017)

Trainings and Retreats
- Tantra Love Retreat, https://www.talktantratome.com/retreat
- International School of Temple Arts (ISTA), https://ista.life/

ALTERNATE RELATING STYLES & SEXUAL ORIENTATION

Books
- *Ace: What Asexuality Reveals about Desire, Society, and the Meaning of Sex,* by Chen, Angela (BEACON PRESS, 2021)
- *Polysecure,* by Fern, Jessica (Scribe Publications, 2022)
- *Sex at Dawn: How We Mate, Why We Stray, and What It Means for Modern Sexuality,* by Ryan, Christopher, and Cacilda Jethŕ. (Scribe Publications, 2021)
- *The Ethical Slut: A Guide to Infinite Sexual Possibilities,* by Easton, Dossie, and Catherine A. Liszt. (Camas Books, 2018)

Online Course
- Love Without Limit, by Frank Mondeose https://www.loveanderos.com/

SHADOW WORK

Books
- *Existential Kink: Unmask Your Shadow and Embrace Your Power,* by Elliott, Carolyn. (Weiser Books, 2020)
- *The Undiscovered Self: The Dilemma of the Individual in Modern Society*, by Jung, C. G., and Hull R F C (Signet, 2006)
- *The Erotic Mind: Unlocking the Inner Sources of Passion and Fulfillment*, by Morin, Jack (HarperCollins, 2012)

SEXUAL ANATOMY & TECHNIQUE

Books
- *Women's Anatomy of Arousal: Secret Maps to Buried Pleasure*, by Winston, Sheri (Mango Garden, 2010)

- *The Multi-Orgasmic Man: Sexual Secrets That Every Man Should Know*, by Chia, Mantak, and Douglas Abrams Arava (Thorsons, 2001)

BDSM & KINK

Online
- The Underline World by Rina Trevi, https://underline.world/

Training
- Tantra Meets BDSM by Om Rupani, https://omrupani.org/tantra-bdsm

THE LAW OF ATTRACTION

Books
- *The Secret,* by Rhonda Byrnes (Atria Books Beyond Words Publishing, 2006)
- *Becoming Supernatural,* by Dr. Joe Dispenza (Hay House Inc, 2019)

FINDING COMMUNITY

Online
- *The Higher Love Club* by Leola, https://www.talktantratome.com/join-hlc
- *Sacred Eros,* an online directory for Tantra and Sacred Sexuality Professionals, https://sacrederos.com/

In-person
- In-person events hosted by Leola in the U.S. and abroad can be found here, https://www.talktantratome.com/events
- Finding in-person, like-minded community is best found by attending local tantra and sex-positive events and spaces. These can be found in Facebook Groups, on Eventbrite, or using Google. If you live in a remote area or in a community that doesn't offer these types of events, I recommend attending a Tantra Retreat or Festival and bringing what you learn back home. If you feel enlivened by this space and inspired to spread these teachings, consider perusing the section below on becoming a professional

in the Sacred Sex and Intimacy Industry. Be the pioneer of such in your local community.

BECOMING A PROFESSIONAL IN THE SACRED SEX AND INTIMACY INDUSTRY

Books
- *Healers on the Edge: Somatic Sex Education*, by Jesse, Moore, and Yahya (Erospirit, 2017)
- *Reclaiming Eros*, by Blackburn, Suzanne (Blue Moon Books, 2011)

Trainings & Retreats
- *Pleasure Priestess Initiation* with Leola, https://www.talktantratome.com/pleasure
- *International School of Temple Arts Practitioner Training*, https://ista.life/trainings/ista-pt
- *Institute of Somatic Sexology*, https://instituteofsomaticsexology.com/
- *Sex and Love University*, https://www.sexandlove.co/university

Becoming a Sacred Intimacy Professional is not a career choice to be taken lightly. If you feel called to this work, please be advised to the importance of being in integrity with your intentions, leaving all ego at the door, and coming from servant leadership. It is important to be trauma informed, to have proper training, and ideally a mentor to support you on the journey. The consequences of not being fully prepared for this career path are dire, as you may seriously hurt someone or yourself without proper care and practice. Unfortunately there are not "boards" for sacred intimacy professionals to ensure all practitioners are in integrity. I am a survivor of sexual assault by a tantra practitioner and know countless others that are laden with controversy because of the unaddressed shadow in their process. Let's not give a bad name to this incredible body of work by creating more trauma and fear from an innocence and naivety that could be prevented.

REFERENCES

- Anderson, L.V. "How Herpes Became a Sexual Boogeyman." *Slate Magazine*, Slate, 2 Dec. 2019, www.slate.com/technology/2019/12/genital-herpes-stigma-history-explained.html.
- Enjara, Luminessa. "Reclaiming the Word Whore." *LinkedIn*, 7 Oct. 2019, www.linkedin.com/pulse/reclaiming-word-whore-luminessa-enjara.
- "Detailed Std Facts - Genital Herpes." *Centers for Disease Control and Prevention*, Centers for Disease Control and Prevention, 22 July 2021, www.cdc.gov/std/herpes/stdfact-herpes-detailed.htm#:~:text=How%20common%20is%20genital%20herpes,States%20in%20a%20single%20year.&text=Nationwide%2C%2011.9%20%25%20of%20persons%20aged,%25%20when%20adjusted%20for%20age).
- "Devastatingly Pervasive: 1 in 3 Women Globally Experience Violence." *World Health Organization*, World Health Organization, www.who.int/news/item/09-03-2021-devastatingly-pervasive-1-in-3-women-globally-experience-violence. Accessed 8 Apr. 2024.
- "Divorce Statistics." *Petrelli Previtera, LLC*, www.petrellilaw.com/divorce-statistics-for-2022/#:~:text=What%20Percent%20of%20Marriages%20End,second%20marriages%20ending%20in%20divorce. Accessed 8 Apr. 2024.
- Fern, Jessica. *Polysecure*. Scribe Publications, 2022.

- "First Council of Nicaea." *Encyclopædia Britannica*, Encyclopædia Britannica, inc., 29 Mar. 2024, www.britannica.com/event/First-Council-of-Nicaea-325.
- Knaus, William A. "'Viruses of Love.'" *The New York Times*, The New York Times, 17 Oct. 1976, www.nytimes.com/1976/10/17/archives/viruses-of-love-one-kind-of-herpes-causes-the-common-cold-sore.html.
- Magazine, Smithsonian. "Who Was Mary Magdalene?" *Smithsonian.Com*, Smithsonian Institution, 1 June 2006, www.smithsonianmag.com/history/who-was-mary-magdalene-119565482/.
- PATTCh. "Birth Trauma: Definition and Statistics." *PATTCh*, 15 Mar. 2022, www.pattch.org/birth-trauma-definition-and-statistics/#:~:text=Between%2025%20and%2034%20per,traumatic(1%2D7). .
- Reed, Amber. "Rewiring the Traumatized, Triune (3 Part) Brain during This Pandemic." *Resolve*, Resolve, 24 Apr. 2020, www.kcresolve.com/blog/rewiring-the-traumatized-triune-3-part-brain-during-this-pandemic.
- Sisowath, Katrina. "The Serpent Priestesses and Ancient Sexual Rites." *Ancient Origins Reconstructing the Story of Humanity's Past*, Ancient Origins, 23 Dec. 2014, www.ancient-origins.net/history/serpent-priestesses-and-ancient-sexual-rites-002491.
- "The Texas Obscenity Law: Penal Code §43.23." *Saputo Toufexis | Criminal Defense*, 22 Mar. 2024, www.saputo.law/criminal-law/texas/obscenity/#:~:text=Texas%20law%20currently%20defines%20the,obscene%20material%20or%20obscene%20device.

www.ingramcontent.com/pod-product-compliance
Lightning Source LLC
Chambersburg PA
CBHW032255150426
43195CB00008BA/465